Transnational Corporations and Poverty Alleviation

By

Eric MULUMBA ZOZO
and
Regis MANKWE BADUZA

Book Cover designer: Francis Lamoste
Printed in USA by CreateSpace

Transnational Corporations and Poverty Alleviation

ISBN-13: 978-0692578162

Printed in the United States of America

DEDICATION

To the Lord God of Israel author of all life

To our relatives and friends

We dedicate this book.

INTRODUCTION

In our lifetime, global poverty has become a morally challenging issue, especially in light of Transnational Corporations (TNCs) economic growth and profitability worldwide this last decade. To tackle the issue of global poverty, different strategies have been suggested. Among these proposed strategies, transnational corporations that export significant financial capital worldwide are presented as a financing method that could contribute to the poverty alleviation. For the proponents of this thesis, transnational corporations have the potential to promote growth and produce a range of social impacts that contribute to poverty reduction.

Neoclassical theories suggest that FDI can be used as a means of bridging the financing gap between desired investments and domestically mobilized savings (Hayami, 2001; Todaro and Smith, 2003). Developing countries are often characterized by high unemployment rate and insufficient capital (local savings). FDI could be a way to address these problems, including bringing foreign capital and increasing production in host countries.

In this view, FDI provides a source of financial capital, complements domestic private investment, increases production, generates new job opportunities, and boosts economic growth in host countries. All of these benefits are expected to promote poverty reduction.

Furthermore, endogenous growth theories suggest that FDI is a mean of technology transfer (Grossman and Helpman, 1991; De Mello, 1997; Borenzstein et al., 1998; Baldwin et al., 2005). This transfer can take place directly through training and improve the local workforce. It may also happen by improving the efficiency of production through imitation and copying technologies, management methods, and organization. Thus, FDI may favor technological progress, stimulate growth and reduce poverty level.

In contrast to this position, FDI might not benefit the poor since TNCs usually recruit skilled workers who are likely to be non-poor. Furthermore, FDI may out-compete local small enterprises making local workers become poor and poor workers further entrenched in poverty. Nevertheless, the impacts of FDI on poverty depend on many factors, including host countries institutions and policies, the quality of the labor market, the economic environment, and the investment itself (Mayne, 1997).

To better comprehend the contribution of TNCs on poverty alleviation, it would be of great interest to review theoretical and empirical arguments on the relationship between FDI and poverty reduction. The aim of this book is to explore mechanisms that link FDI and poverty, potential FDI effects on poverty reduction and to find strategies that can be used to better enhance TNCs contribution to poverty reduction.

Chapter 1

Transnational Corporations

Transnational Corporations

A transnational corporation is one that engages in foreign direct investment (FDI) and owns or, in some way, controls value-added activities in more than one country (Dunning and Lundan, 2008).

Transnational Corporation capital exported from one country to the rest of the world is often measured by

FDI. However, this is a partial measure of the evolution of TNCs abroad because a firm establishing a plant or an office in a foreign country can expand without capital export from the home country by borrowing locally or reinvesting its profits. Nevertheless, FDI is one of the most important indicators to assess TNC activities overseas.

For many people, TNCs have come to symbolize what is wrong with globalization; many would say they are a primary cause of its problems. These companies are richer than most countries in the developing world. In 2004, the revenues of U.S. car company General Motors were $191.4 billion, greater than the GDP of more than 148 countries. In its fiscal year ending in 2005, U.S. retailer Walmart's revenues were $285.2 billion, larger than the combined GDP of sub-Saharan Africa. These corporations are not only rich but politically powerful. Multinational corporations, at the center of globalization, can be blamed for much of its ills as well as given credit for many of its achievements (Stiglitz, 2007).

In the past, TNCs activities through FDI had sometimes outcompeted local small enterprises and provoked job destruction. Nonetheless, many empirical studies show that through FDI, TNCs have repeatedly reduced unemployment rate, increase production, and favor new transfer technology in host countries. This leads us to say that the debate on the role of TNCs in poverty reduction through FDI is still open to discussion.

Foreign Direct Investment (FDI)

Moosa (2002) defines Foreign Direct Investment (FDI) as a process where enterprises residing in a country (mother country) acquire property assets in another country (host country) in order to control production, distribution or any other activities in this country. The OECD defines the operations of foreign direct investment as follows:

> "Foreign direct investment reflects the objective of obtaining a lasting interest by a resident entity in one economy (''direct investor'') in an entity resident in an economy other than that of the investor (''direct investment enterprise''). The lasting interest implies the existence of a long-term relationship between the direct investor and the enterprise and a significant degree of influence on the management of the enterprise.

Direct investment involves both the initial transaction between the two entities and all subsequent capital transactions between them and among affiliated enterprises, both incorporated and unincorporated."[1]

FDI is defined by the World Bank as an investment made to acquire a lasting management in an enterprise operating in a country other than that of the investor. In general, investment that includes at least a 10 percent ownership of an enterprise is considered as FDI.

The foreign direct investment concept is characterized by the contribution of a foreign firm in decision-making in a local company. This refers to the concept of control manifested, particularly through the involvement in the board of directors and the appointment of leaders (Moosa, 2002). An investment must also have a long-term relationship reflecting a certain interest in the evolutionary control of the enterprise residing in the host country. The durability of this control is essential to distinguish between FDI and portfolio investment. The latter is motivated by short-term profits and often made for reasons of speculation.

1. http://www.oecd.org/dataoecd/10/16/2090148.pdf

Why do companies interested in an international market not use all their skills and assets to produce and export in their countries? Why do companies invest abroad? The answer to these questions comes from the study of different FDI theories.

Several theories provide some answers to these questions. Dunning (1977) formulated the O.L.I paradigm, which explains the decisions in favor of foreign investments through three advantages: ownership, location, and internationalization.

New trade theories have built upon this paradigm by incorporating ideas developed by the neoclassical theory of international trade as well as those developed by the industrial economies. This has led to the theory of two approaches, each arguing for a particular strategy of FDI. Thus, FDI can have market-seeking strategies which correspond to horizontal FDI and minimization of costs strategies, which corresponds to vertical FDI.

FDI with Horizontal Strategy

Horizontal or marked strategies apply to decisions of foreign investment aimed at producing both for local consumption and for the host market (Michalet, 1999).

Michalet also stipulates that horizontal FDI strategies are made in countries that have equivalent levels of development. Strategy can be described as horizontal as it relates to cross-investment flows that develop between the United States, Europe and Japan, within the triad. Most studies agree that FDI is primarily horizontal. Markusen (1995) explains the existence of horizontal FDI by developing two types of approaches.

First, macroeconomic approaches show that the differences between endowments of production factors do not account for the largest share of FDI. Contrarily, FDI with horizontal strategies move between countries with similar incomes, similar factors of endowments, and low barriers to international trade.

Second, microeconomic approaches indicate that TNCs play an important role in industries that have a high level of research and development relative to sales. TNCs are also active where investments in structures of employment are concentrated in skilled and semi-skilled labor. In this category of FDI, the value of intangible assets the market value without the value of tangible assets is very important.

FDI with Vertical Strategy

The vertical strategy of FDI, unlike the horizontal strategy, represents flows that are exclusively directed from the North to the South. Here, developing countries do not invest in countries of the triad and the flows are unidirectional (Michalet, 1999). This strategy is mainly based on inter-branch trade according to the theory of international trade. The differences of production costs in endowment factors (capital and labor) and comparative advantages of countries play an important role in the explanation of vertical FDI (HOS model).

Hanson et al. (2001) and Braconier et al. (2002) state that FDI with a vertical strategy tries to reduce production costs through differences in factors of prices. FDIs that have a vertical strategy are the result of the international division of the value chain. The top of the scale of the value chain is intensive in physical capital or technology, while the bottom is intensive in unskilled labor. Helpman (1984) demonstrated that when differences in factor prices between countries are important, TNCs locate their labor in countries where labor costs are relatively low.

Economic models explain that vertical and horizontal FDIs impose many restrictions on behavior of TNCs. In reality, as Baltagi et al. (2008) affirm, a firm can simultaneously invest in one country as a market strategy and in another country as a cost reduction strategy. These investments characterize complex or hybrid integration strategies.

Several African countries are major destinations for FDI. These countries are coveted for the exploitation of their natural resources. This strategy is a special case of vertical FDI that we will consider below.

Natural Resources FDI Strategy

The primary reason for FDI attractiveness was the strategy for access to natural resources. Since it appeared even before the concept of "Globalization," it is not solely a feature of the multinational or global economy (Michalet, 1999). Natural resources have two components: non-renewable natural resources on one hand, such as oil, natural gas and various minerals (coal, copper, nickel) and renewable natural resources on the other hand, such as wood, various crops, fishing, and agricultural products. Overall, the two types of natural resources differ from other sectors by three aspects (McKern 1993).

First, for reasons related to geology and climatology, natural resources are characterized by a geographical immobility. Their distribution is skewed in terms of technology, resources, and markets. In fact, much of these resources are located in the South, while the largest markets are in the North. Similarly, technologies from developed countries are needed to exploit these resources, which are mastered by large firms in developed countries. Second, FDI in natural resources are characterized by a large capital intensive with large economies of scale. Finally, several studies emphasize the high concentration of supply of nonrenewable natural resources (Vernon 1971).

Factors that promote FDI that focus on natural resources were identified by Vernon (1971). In the exploitation of mineral and energy products, FDI are not only attracted to the minimization of cost or market research. They are also motivated by reasons of precaution, diversification and risk reduction dependen cies. To do this, TNCs have a two-fold objective: to secure supplies that are not dependent on competitors and diversify the number of suppliers so as to avoid dependency. In addition, factors that discourage FDI in natural resources are the existence of political risk and lack of infrastructure.

In summary, there are different types of FDI: horizontal, vertical, and natural resources-oriented. Developing countries covet these investments because of their needs, their markets and their endowment factors. Thus, they hope to take advantage of FDI to promote growth and reduce poverty in their countries.

Chapter 2

Poverty

Poverty is a complex phenomenon. Indeed, in the literature, a single universally accepted definition of poverty does not exist. Poverty is usually defined in relation to income in terms of gross domestic product (GDP) per capita. Extreme poverty is often defined as an income of less than $1 a day per person in terms of purchasing power parity (PPP). Some researchers define poverty in terms of GDP or PPP, which does not fully capture the phenomenon of poverty. A broader definition treats poverty as multidimensional, including (i) low income, (ii) low levels of education and health, (iii) vulnerability (to health or income loss, natural disaster, crime and violence, and education curtailment) and (iv) voicelessness and powerlessness (feeling discrimination, lacking income earning possibilities, mistreatment by state institutions, and lacking status under the law) (World Bank, 2001).

Poverty can be perceived from two different angles: individual poverty and widespread or mass poverty. Individual poverty characterizes the situation of a person or a small portion of the population living on the margin of a moderately prosperous society. The study of individual poverty is primarily microeconomic in nature, but it can also be the object of social, anthropological, and cultural studies. This poverty is related to the behavior of each individual and is at the center of neoclassical theories as well as individualistic and utilitarian approaches.

Mass poverty characterizes an entity or group residing in the same geographical area and having ethnic background with cultural and social similarities. Widespread poverty affects a community, a country or a region. According to Paugman (2005), mass poverty characterizes economically "backward" countries and is manifested by the existence of a large informal sector. Given its overall appearance, mass poverty is often explained by macroeconomic factors and is at the center of theories of developmental economics. Poverty within these countries is not synonymous with exclusion and the poor are not necessarily stigmatized.

An individual or a group of individuals are considered poor when they have no access to a minimum level of requirements corresponding to primary or basic needs. This definition raises some questions about the terms "access," "minimal," and "basic needs."

The analysis of concepts inherent to the definition of poverty has given rise to two economic approaches: the absolute approach and the relative approach.

Absolute Poverty

Absolute poverty theory was initiated in 1899 by the Seebohm Rowntree study on poverty in England. While collecting detailed information on the York population, Rowntree defined people lacking sufficient income to obtain the indispensable elements for the physical efficiency. He evaluated the poverty line based on average nutritional needs by adding a minimum of expenditure on clothing and housing, and by taking into account household size (Townsend, 1979).

Taking into consideration the study of Ahluwalia et al. (1979), the World Bank conducted a study on poverty in the 12 poorest countries to make an international threshold in 1985. The study shows that the thresholds in these countries were similar and equivalent to $ 370 a year per person (Shiller, 2008). This line is very close to the level of $ 365, and it has been likened to the "dollar a day" theory. Thus, the poverty line of 1 dollar per day appears to be essential for obtaining the basket containing the basic minimum of calories. Anyone living below this threshold is considered to be in extreme poverty.

This standard defines extreme poverty or absolute poverty. Several criticisms on the absolute poverty approach were raised to relate methods of adjustment and definition of the basket of basic needs. The absolute poverty level is adjusted only by taking inflation into account. Yet, the notion of basic need is not fixed. It is dependent upon individual, cultural and regional preferences. Similarly, the number of calories required for subsistence of an individual may not be the same for another individual. Rather, it depends on the energy expenditure that a person is capable of spending and their living conditions. In good weather, 1000 kcal would be sufficient for the survival of an inert man. In more severe climatic conditions or in companies where individuals are forced to perform a given work, at least 3000 kcal would be necessary for survival (Townsend, 1979).

Basic needs are beyond materialist conception of an individual. Furthermore, as human beings, happiness and well-being of individuals depend on their economic, social, political, cultural, and spiritual needs. Thus, the approach of absolute poverty cannot in any way accurately reflect the magnitude of social exclusion or marginalization around the world. The weaknesses of the absolute approach have led economists and sociologists to develop a relative approach.

Relative Poverty

Relative poverty can be defined as the minimum necessary for the survival of an individual, both physically and socially. Therefore, it is somewhat subjective. Furthermore, in a monetary approach, a person is considered poor if his or her income is significantly lower than the average or the population median. Thus, the measure of poverty avoids the problem of defining basic needs and focuses on the distribution of wealth while reflecting on a quest for equity in economic and social participation (Atkinson, 1998).

In reality, both approaches to poverty are used in developed and developing countries. The measure of absolute poverty is still used in the United States and Canada, countries in which social success is solely dependent on individuals' actions. Similarly, the concept of relative poverty can be used in African countries where much of the population does not feel relatively poor. In fact, the coexistence of these two approaches demonstrates their complementarity. According to Atkinson (1998), the absolute poverty approach reflects the need for a minimum "standard of living" so that the approach reflects a vision of "minimum fee."

Amarytha Sen, Nobel laureate in economics, criticized this relative-absolute dichotomy, which defines poverty through a concept linking product attributes to their use and to the satisfaction they give to individuals. Sen (1983) shows that access to a property is not sufficient to describe its use. Sen uses the approach of "capability" to overcome the conflict between the concepts of relative and absolute poverty (Bourguignon, 2003). Indeed, poverty is an absolute notion in the sense of "capability," but takes on a relative dimension when it is specific to properties. Thus, the poverty line determined monetarily has no sense in this approach.

Sen's approach has had much influence on new definitions of poverty. The lack of monetary indicators has prompted the search for alternative indicators reflecting the notion of "capability." Thus, non-monetary measures can cover the multidimensional nature of poverty. They describe factors related to health, education, social relations, security and vulnerability.

Nevertheless, given the need to compare, verify, and assess poverty and the political struggle against poverty, it is important to use methods of measurement that are appropriate to the nature of qualitative non-monetary indicators. Fixing a threshold will depend on the nature of the measures chosen. This has led to the emergence of human development indicators.

Poverty has often been the subject of several economic, political, sociological, anthropological, religious, and others studies. It should be noted that all social sciences contain a debate between two visions of the main causes of poverty: an individualistic approach and a structuralist view.

The first, the individualistic view puts the responsibility for poverty on the poor themselves by showing that their situation is the result of their actions, laziness, incapacity and irrationality.

The individualist vision is inspired on capitalism. It focuses on economic and political failures of poor countries. This vision focuses on market mechanisms of poverty reduction and shows that international financial aid is inefficient and only exacerbates the dependency of poor countries. Thus, it suggests free trade, encourages private investment and the reduction of government intervention in the economy as a means of promoting development. Furthermore, international aid can be negatively perceived in the sense that it could encourage the creation of a poverty trap.

The stucturalistic view puts the responsibility of the existence of poverty on errors, inconsistencies, and injustices established on economic, political or social systems. The structuralist vision comes from Marxist or the socialist vision. It denies the validity of liberal theories and focuses on the injustice of the global economy, free trade, and the misjudgments of the Bretton Woods institutions toward poor countries.

Since the fall of the Berlin Wall (1989) and the failure of recommendations of dependency theories in several countries, FDI has been regarded as an engine of growth and is eagerly sought by countries seeking development. Nevertheless, does it mean that FDI is a universal remedy for poverty reduction?

In the following chapters, we will review and analyze theoretical and empirical arguments of FDI effects on economic growth and poverty reduction.

Chapter 3

Institutional Mechanisms of FDI Effects on Poverty

In recent years, theories of new institutional economics (Matthews, 1986) have taken a central place in development models. These theories emphasize the importance of institutions[2] in the process of poverty

2. In the literature, the concepts of "institutions" broadly refer to the activities of the state in a country with the objective of ensuring individual and global well-being. Institutions

reduction. Thus, studies of institutional mechanisms of FDI effects on poverty can be divided into two parts: the impact of FDI on institutions and the way FDI can affect the redistribution of income.

Effects of FDI on Institutions

In theoretical and empirical literature, no consensus has been reached concerning the impact of FDI on local institutions. Thus, arguments that suggest both positive and perverse effects of FDI may be found.

According to Acemoglu et al. (2005), interactions between economic and political powers produce and change institutions. Within economic actors, TNCs play a very important role. Indeed, these companies, which are generally larger than local firms have strong bargaining power with public authorities (Bastos and Nasir, 2004). This power flows from the strategic importance of the sector in which they operate (natural resources), the importance of the employed workforce (manufacturing) and the intensity of fall back technology.

---

functioning are referred to as "governance." In what follows, we will use these expressions interchangeably.

When FDI productivity depends on the quality of the investment climate and institutions, TNCs use their bargaining power to encourage the state to make necessary administrative reforms. In this case, TNCs act positively to enhance the regularization of institutions (Xu and Shenkar, 2002). According to Dollar et al. (2006), the pressure exerted by the government on TNCs is larger when FDI is focused on manufacturing export activities. This is manifested by the creation of exporters lobby for improved infrastructure, trade liberalization, and reduction of bureaucracy. Similarly, it has been shown that FDIs in manufacturing move to countries where the investment climate is initially positive (Gorg and Greenway, 2003).

Although FDI can help improve institutions' economic efficiency, TNCs can backfire in some cases. Indeed, Johnson et al. (2007) show that when revenues from foreign trade or FDI fall into the hands of undemocratic governments, it may lead to a concentration of power and can therefore affect institutions. Hence, the productivity of TNCs located in countries with bad institutions is relatively independent of regulatory, normative, and cognitive components of institutions (Xu and Shenkar, 2002). In this case, the profitability of TNCs only depends on exogenous factors, including the abundance of natural resources. Conversely, in order to receive the rent of natural resources, predatory states are encouraged to create distortions in institutions. This is manifested by the concentration of power, the interference in the functioning of the legal and informational opacity. This was particularly demonstrated in the work of Collier and Gunning (1999), Isham et al. (2003) and Collier (2007).

FDI, Institutions, and Redistribution of Income

For some authors, there is a relationship between FDI, institutional quality, and the level of inequality and poverty. According to Johnson et al. (2007), institutions make all laws, rules, and practices that govern property rights. They have the duty to provide general order, public safety, as well as private and bureaucratic efficiency. Therefore, as stated in North's definition (1990), institutions play an important role in maintaining harmonious balances between different society components, without necessarily ensuring equality between them. In this regard, institutions determine how individuals can earn a daily income, enter in contact with other economic actors, exchange goods and services, as well as obtain material resources necessary for their economic sustenance.

Several studies have shown the crucial importance of good institutions[3] in the allocation of income beneficial to poor people (Kaufman et al., 1999; Rodrik et al., 2004; Acemoglu and Robinson, 2008). Indeed, good institutions promote an effective protection of political, civil and human rights of citizens in accordance with the rule of law providing effective and non-corrupted public services to the people and utilizing public resources in an accountable and transparent way with the aim of promoting general social welfare. It has become increasingly apparent that there is a vital connection between open, democratic, and accountable systems of governance and the ability to achieve sustained economic and social development (Neumayer, 2003).

In contrast, prior research shows that in several countries where bad institutions[4] exist, weak governance

---

3. The term "good institutions" refers to institutions that favor democracy, reduce corruption, and reinforce stability (Rodrik et al., 2004).
4. Bad Institutions refers to institutions that do not favor democracy and maintain corruption, mismanagement and instability.

reinforces poverty. Kaufman found a significant causal relationship between the rule of law and the nations' income, as well as with reduced infant mortality and literacy (Kaufman et al., 1999). After conducting a study in 60 countries, Narayan et al. (2000) found that the common element that ties the poor together was the lack of power and voice. In fact, the impact of poor standards of governance usually falls most heavily on the poor.

Furthermore, when the initial quality of institutions is weak, some TNC strategies can strengthen bad governance, reducing the potential for development. This approach is explained by the phenomenon of "political Dutch disease," which means a political system that tends to suffocate any competitor (Lam & Wantchekon, 2003). Thus, FDI attracted to the discovery of new natural resources can affect institutions so as to create political and economic blockades.

The relationship between inequality and institutions has a character of reciprocal causality. According to Johnson et al. (2007), the existence of inequalities in society negatively affects the quality of institutions in promoting economic and political leadership. Indeed, a company with strong inequalities creates institutions biased in favor of political or economic elites (Acemoglu et al., 2005). Subsequently, these institutions will exacerbate the level of inequality and increase exclusion. Thus, inequality and institutions interact to create a vicious circle. Breaking this circle would be the duty of a change, especially from an autonomous will.

Chapter 4

Microeconomic Mechanisms of FDI Effects on Poverty

The microeconomic approach studies the direct effects of FDI on poverty through employment creation and analysis of relationships between local firms and TNCs. A major question is to find out how FDI contributes to the reduction of existing unemployment and underemployment rates, providing people with income and therefore directly contributing to poverty reduction.

To answer this question, it is interesting to see how the entry of TNCs in an economy can create jobs and generate stimulatory effects or crowd out local firms. Indeed, to be efficient, job creation given in the host country should be more important than job destruction due to the use of FDI (layoff due to mergers and acquisitions, closing of local firms, etc.).

FDI's direct impact on poverty works through its effects on employment since the entry of foreign capital does not replace local investment. In this sense, foreign investment takes the mode of green-field investment[5] and may contribute to reducing underemployment and unemployment. Thus, by providing new income, FDI directly contributes to the reduction of poverty. This has been considered as a major impact of FDI on poverty (Chudnovsky and López, 1999; Saravanamuttoo, 1999).

Conversely to Green-field enterprises, FDI may raise unemployment when it is a merge-and-acquisition (M&A) activity. This is because M&A activities are usually followed by restructuring merged enterprise in

---

5. Green-field investments occur when multinational corporations enter into developing countries to build new factories and/or stores.

accordance with the objectives underlying the M&A (UNCTAD, 1999, p. 261). However, when FDI takes the mode of merge-and-acquisition of moribund enterprises it may help to potentially increase unemployment and therefore poverty. In other situations, foreign investors may preempt investment opportunities for any local firms. The resulting direct unemployment impact may not be of great value since similar results would have occurred otherwise.

Besides M&A, confronting domestic supply with new foreign supply may create foreclosure effects through competitive mechanisms (Aitken and Harrison, 1999). Competition between local firms and TNCs can have destructive effects on the local economy. As Bienayme (1998) noted, when large companies enter a market that is still in its infancy, they can destroy a still nascent and fragile supply structure. Indeed, TNCs have a clear superiority in technology, finance, and production processes (internalization advantages). To operate a market, they are often looking for monopoly rents. In this case, FDI may out-compete local firms, consequently increase unemployment and causing local workers become poor and poor workers worse.

The economic literature presents two main cases where competition may favor foreclosure effects. The first case can be seen in market for products when TNCs prevent local firms from acquiring knowledge and skills needed for their production (Markussen and Venable, 1999). The second case can be observed in the factor market when TNCs limit the access of local businesses to resources and funding needed (Borsworth and Collins, 1999). Local firms that will not withstand the force of TNCs will disappear from the market. This competition affects FDI strategies, both horizontally and vertically.

The literature mentions that FDI effects on poverty not only work to increase the employment rate, but also the quality of employment. The location of created employment is a concern as well. TNCs may reduce underemployment in host countries by offering jobs with higher pay and better working conditions. FDI in low wage, low-skill labor industries with or without negligibly upgrading human capital may help only to reduce poverty in the short-run. In fact, this kind of FDI locks workers in a low-skill state and can easily move to new places with lower labor costs, thereby quitting employees become a common occurrence. Thus, it is not only that employment is offered to the poor, but also that the type of employment being created and the sustainability of the employment are also of relevance to aid poor people.

The location of employment created through FDI seems to be of direct importance to poverty reduction. TNCs may directly raise income in, loosely speaking, poor areas that is those with high unemployment or underemployment rates. Likewise, in cases where FDI stimulate migration of domestic investors to poor areas with widespread unemployment or underemployment rates, it is considered to reduce poverty as well. However, these effects seem to rarely occur, except in the case of resource-seeking FDI or when host governments have policies that promote investment to exploit excess labor supply in such areas. To the extent that FDIs are allocated to congested urban areas with good infrastructures, it may just worsen income distribution and its implication on poverty may seem to be negligible. In the same way, TNCs that crowd out local producers in poor areas by their competiveness or by reliance on imports adversely affect poverty (Nguyen, 2003).

The relationship between TNCs and local firms are the micro side of the effects of FDI on the labor market and subsequently the structure of poverty. Indeed, through the process of production and marketing, TNCs interact with local firms. In this context, they can either displace local businesses or stimulate them. In doing so, they affect the demand for labor in terms of quality, quantity and wages. This has an undeniable effect on poverty reduction. In a macroeconomic approach, this relationship becomes the study of mechanisms through which FDI affects economic growth and therefore poverty.

Chapter 5

Macroeconomic Mechanisms of FDI Effects on Growth and Poverty

The macroeconomic approach studies indirect effects of FDI on poverty through economic growth. FDI has the potential of being an engine of economic growth that can have positive impacts on poverty reduction. FDI that impact poverty through growth are inherently difficult to measure. However, theoretically, FDI can mainly reduce poverty in recipient countries through three different ways. First, FDI can affect poverty through capital inflows by increasing production. Second, poverty can be affected through the allocation of tax revenue collected from foreign firms to economic activities that benefit the poor directly or indirectly. Third, FDI can contribute to poverty reduction through the transfer of new technologies, knowledge, and other intangible assets.

1. Through capital inflows by increasing production, growth and employment creation

Neoclassical theories show that FDI is a mean of bridging financing gap by using foreign capital and capital accumulation. Developing countries are often characterized by high unemployment rate and insufficient capital (local savings). FDI could be a way of addressing these problems, including bringing foreign capital and increasing the production in host countries. In this sense, FDI can be considered as an engine of growth. Overall, this follows from the growth models of Harrod and Domar, influenced by Keynesian's thinking, and the theoretical contribution of Chenery and Strout that extend the original model to the case of developing countries.

In this context, TNC performance can contribute to the stimulation of economic growth by promoting both forward and backward production linkages with domestic industries and other sectors. For instance, in subcontracting systems between TNCs and local subcontractors who supply spare parts, components, or semi-finished goods to TNCs, additional employment is indirectly created. In this view, FDI can contribute to stimulating economic growth and job creation that will promote poverty reduction.

The ultimate impact of FDI on economic growth in host countries depends not only on the performance of TNCs which increase production, but also on the diffusion of new technologies, innovations, knowledge, new best practices and other intangible assets from FDI throughout the economy of the host countries.

2: Through Transfer of New Technology, Knowledge, and Other Intangible Assets

With the advent of theories of endogenous growth, FDI is now considered a mean of technology transfer (Grossman and Helpman, 1991; Borensztein et al., 1998; De Mello, 1999; Baldwin et al., 2005; Barro, 2001). Thus, opportunities to promote technological progress in host countries positively depend on agglomeration effects (Brainard, 1997) and the technological gap (Lucas, 1988). However, these opportunities can be inhibited when human capital in a host country is inadequate. This concerns thresholds effects (Pissarides, 1997, De Mello, 1999; Borensztein et al., 1998).

The transfer of knowledge can take many forms. First, TNCs can play the role of "demonstrator incentive" for local businesses. They constitute a new channel to export or learning that occurs through observation (Blomstrom et al., 2000). Second, some authors, including Jenkins and Thomas (2002) focus on technology transfer through the movement of workers between foreign firms and local firms. Furthermore, knowledge transfer can take place through imitation and copying technologies, management methods and organization to improve the production efficiency.

According to Rodrik (1999) as well as Gorg and Greenaway (2003), manufacturing FDI particularly favors this type of transfer. However, the degree and quality of imitation depend on the complexity of the processes of origin. Indeed, it reduces the chances of local firms to imitate foreign companies.

While TNCs can stimulate growth through technological progress, the process requires the existence of certain conditions. According to Blomstrom and Kokko (1996), the transfer depends on the absorptive capacity of local firms, which themselves depends on the level of development reached by the host country, the qualification of the local workforce and the existence of a capital human threshold.

3: Through the Allocation of Tax Revenue Collected from Foreign Firms

The third way that FDI can have a positive effect on poverty reduction is through taxation of foreign subsidiaries, that raises government revenues, which in turn can be used to fund various social development programs, including productive improvement and development of labor-intensive economic activities (such as industry and agriculture) or poverty alleviation oriented projects (Diagram 5).

However, whether this type of indirect benefit from FDI on poverty alleviation in host countries can be realized depending on at least three pre-conditions. First, tax systems in the host countries should be attractive for investment, including foreign investment. If, for instance, corporate tax rates in host countries are too high as compared to other potential countries for FDI, it may deter foreign investment. Internationally compatible corporate tax rates should reduce incentives to engage in "transfer pricing," a practice which reduces tax revenue in the host's economy. Second, whether or not government budgets gain sufficiently from taxing foreign subsidiaries depends on what policies and agreements are in place to ensure that tax revenue and royalties are actually collected.

In reality, this is not always the case, as foreign firms often use transfer pricing to minimize tax burden. UNCTAD (1999) notes that reforms to restrictions on profit remittance and double taxation treaties should have reduced the use of transfer pricing to withdraw income from the host economy. But in the report, it is argued that this issue remains a concern for developing countries. For instance, it appears from a study conducted by

UNCTAD that about 84% of developing countries participating in a survey believed that affiliate companies hosted in their economy shifted income to parent firms in order to reduce tax liabilities. The study concluded that transfer pricing continues to be an issue, with action required at both the national level and in the context of international investment arrangements (Jenkins and Thomas, 2002). Third, collected taxes from FDI is used to finance employment creation or poverty alleviation oriented programs or projects such as development of labor-intensive projects or small and medium enterprises. In addition, it can be used to support the development of a safety net for the poor or to finance imports of components or raw materials for domestic capital-intensive industries.

The economic literature is very rich in the treatment of the relationship between growth and FDI. Through models of capital stock expansion, endogenous growth, and collected tax revenues, we learn that the implementation of TNCs in a country is an argument in favor of economic growth. However, the Dutch disease model warns us about the possible negative effects of FDI in natural resources on industrialization and growth.

Furthermore, empirical studies of FDI impacts on growth give mixed results.

Chapter 6

Empirical Studies on the impacts of FDI on Growth

Several research studies have been devoted to the causality direction between FDI and economic growth using a number of econometric techniques. Findings from these studies are mixed and can be grouped in three categories. The first group of studies suggests that FDI does increase growth. The second group of studies establishes negative effects of FDI on growth. The last group of studies reports both positive and negative effects of FDI on economic growth. In this section we review selected empirical studies which report the results set above and we address some limitations of prior research related to the subject.

Positive Effects of FDI on Growth

Among recent popular and influential work are Borensztein et al. (1998) who tested the effect of FDI on economic growth in a framework of cross-country regressions for 69 developing countries over the last decade using endogenous growth model. Their results suggest that FDI does indeed play an important role in the transfer of technology, leading to growth in larger measure than domestic investment. Their results indicate that an increase of one percent in the ratio of FDI to GDP increases the GDP growth rate per capita of the host country by 0.8 percent. In addition, the authors found a strong complementary effect between FDI and human capital, that is, the contribution of FDI to economic growth was enhanced by its interaction with the level of human capital in the host country. Earlier works by Bulasubramanyam et al. (1996) examined the relationship between FDI and growth in the context of differing trade policy regimes, i.e., export, promoting, and import substituting countries. Using cross section data to analyze 46 developing countries over the period of 1970-1985, it was found that Bhagwati's hypothesis supports that FDI will increase growth in countries which adopt export promotion policy.

De Mello (1999) attempted to find support for FDI led growth hypothesis with time series analysis and panel data estimation for a sample of 32 OECD and non-OECD countries covering the period of 1970-1990. In the first case, De Mello began his Granger causality test by a test for stationarity, after which he verifies the short and long term relationship between two variables with a normal test (co-integration), and finally ends his analysis with a test on panel data. The author found that FDI had a positive impact on output growth and also that there was a dominant complementarity effect between FDI and domestic investment.

Campos and Kinoshita (2002) examined the effects of FDI on growth for the period between 1990 and 1998, for 25 Central and Eastern European and former Soviet Union transition economies. In these countries FDI consisted of pure technology transfer. Their main results indicated that FDI had a significant positive effect on the economic growth of each selected country. These results were consistent with the theory that equates FDI with technology transfers from which the host country benefits.

Over the period of 1987-1997, Wang (2002) used panel data from 12 Asian economies and found that total FDI inflows significantly affect economic growth. Disaggregating the types of flows entering these economies, she found that only FDI in the manufacturing sector had a significant and positive impact on economic growth and attributed this positive contribution to FDIs spillover effects.

Bengoa et al. (2003) estimated the relationship between FDI and economic growth using panel data for 18 Latin American countries over the period of 1970-1999. They showed that FDI had positive and significant impact on economic growth in host countries. However, as in most other papers, Bengoa et al. (2003) found that the benefit to the host country requires adequate human capital, political and economic stability and liberalized market environment.

Similarly, Marwah and Tavakoli (2004) tested the effect of FDI on economic growth in Indonesia, Malaysia, Philippines, and Thailand. Using time series annual data over the period of 1970-1998, they found that FDI had a positive correlation with economic growth for all four countries.

Hansen and Rand (2006) re-examine the causal links between FDI and economic growth in 31 developing countries over a period of 31 years (1970-2000). They used bivariate vector VAR models for GDP and FDI ratios. They found a strong causal connection between FDI and GDP, even in the long run.

Vu et al. (2006) studied sector-specific FDI inflows for both China over the period of 1985-2002 and Vietnam over the period 1990-2002. Using an augmented production function specification and regression methodology, they concluded that FDI had both positive and direct impact on economic growth as well as an indirect effect through its impact on labor productivity.

Alfaro and Charlton (2007), made a distinction between the different "qualities" of FDI in order to re-examine the relationship between growth and FDI. In their study, 'quality' means the effect of a unit of FDI on economic growth. Exploiting a new comprehensive industry-level data set of 29 countries between 1985 and 2000, they found that when they account for the quality of FDI, growth effects of FDI also increased. After controlling for industry characteristics and time effects, they found the relationship between FDI and economic growth to no longer be ambiguous but rather positive and significant.

Pertaining to regional analysis, Apergis et al. (2007) examined the impact of FDI on economic growth using regression analysis on panel data set from 27 European transitional economies over the period of 1991-2004. Their empirical findings reveal that FDI indicate evidence of a significant positive linkage with economic growth, at least, for transitional countries that have implemented successful privatization programs and are characterized by high levels of income.

Table 1: Positive Effects of FDI on Growth

Author (Year)	Methodology	Findings
Bulasubramanyam et al. (1996)	Estimation using cross section data to analyze regimes of 46 developing countries over the period of 1970-1985 in the context of differing trade policies.	They found support for Bhagwati's hypothesis that FDI increases growth in countries that adopt export promotion policies.
Borensztein et al. (1998)	Estimation of the effect of FDI on economic growth in a framework of cross-country regressions for 69 developing countries over the last decade using endogenous growth model.	An increase of one percent in the ratio of FDI to GDP increases the GDP growth rate per capita of the host country by 0.8 percent.
De Mello (1999)	Time series analysis and panel data estimation for a sample of 32 OECD and non - OECD countries covering the period of 1970-1990.	He found a positive impact on output growth and that there was a dominant complementarity effect between FDI and domestic investment.
Vu et al. (2006)	Production function specification and regression methodology. For both China over the period of 1985-2002 and Vietnam over the period of 1990-2002.	They found that FDI has positive and direct impact on economic growth as well as an indirect effect through its impact on labor productivity.

Author (Year)	Methodology	Findings
Alfaro and Charlton (2007)	Exploiting a new comprehensive industry level data set of 29 countries between 1985 and 2000.	They found that when they account for the quality of FDI, the growth effects of FDI increase also. They found the positive and significant effect.

Mixed Effects of FDI on Growth

Certain empirical studies established negative or mixed effects of FDI on growth. Kholdy (1995) carries out Granger causality tests, using data from 10 East Asian economies, but does not find a causative link between FDI and productivity. Carkovic and Levine (2002) as well as Nair-Reichert and Weinhold (2001) criticize research that is based on heterogeneous samples. This skews the results and leads to a distortion of policy recommendations. By means of a panel method, they found that there is a highly heterogeneous causal relationship between FDI and growth. Carkovic and Levine (2002) make use of different countries and analyzed a data sample of 72 countries, ranging from America to Africa that includes aggregate FDI flows to each of the countries. The results of their analyses show that exogenous components of FDI have no effect on growth. Indeed, FDI lose their significance when authors take into account the regression of trade openness, the exchange rate of informal market and financial development indicators. This is due to the existence of a strong endogeneity between these variables and FDI.

In this sense, Nair-Reichert and Weinhold (2001) conducted an econometric study that used the Holtz-Eakin causality test on a panel of 24 developing countries between 1971 and 1995. They found no causal relationship between FDI and growth. Nair-Reichert and Weinhold (2001) as well as Narayan and Pritchett (1997), show that the effect of FDI on growth in poor countries is independent of the quality of human capital due to the existence of threshold effects.

Zhang (2001) did some research to determine the meaning of the relationship between FDI and growth in 11 Asian and Latin America countries. He uses the unique time series for each country and conducted causality tests for a long period based on error correction model. The results show that there is no relationship between FDI and growth in Argentina in the short and long term while a relationship between growth and FDI exists in Brazil in the short term and in Columbia in the long term. Concerning Asian countries, the author found a short-term causal relationship from growth to FDI in Korea, Malaysia, and Thailand. In total, in five of the 11 countries studied, growth is accelerated by FDI. For six countries, there is no co-integration relationship between FDI and growth; only one country showed a causal relationship between growth and FDI.

Katerina et al. (2004) examined the effects of Foreign Direct Investment (FDI) on economic growth mainly focusing on the US and western European countries. They investigated the existence and the nature of the effect of FDI on the rate of growth of a panel of 17 transition economies. They applied Bayesian analysis and their results indicated that FDI does not exhibit any significant relationship with economic growth in transition countries.

Bosworth and Collins (1999) evaluated the implications of capital inflows in the form of FDI, portfolio investment and bank loans in 58 developing countries during the period of 1978-1995, and the uses made of these flows. These countries were located in

Latin America, Asia, and Africa. Most of the inflows were concentrated in Asia and Latin America for the period of 1990-1995. The authors used regression analysis on panel data. They examined the effect of capital inflows on investment and saving, measured as percentages of GDP. Their results indicated that total capital inflows had a positive effect on investment, while they had an insignificant negative effect on the saving rate.

Agosin and Mayer (2000) found mixed effects of FDI on growth by conducting their study by region using a sample smaller than Bosworth and Collins' research (32 countries) but for a longer period (1970-1996). These authors found that an increase of one dollar of invested FDI leads to an increase of more than a dollar total investment (crowding in) in Asia, meaning that FDI stimulated domestic investment in Asia. In contrast, FDI led to crowding out effects in Latin America, while FDI impacts were neutral in Africa overall, although Ivory Coast, Ghana, and Senegal still seemed to have benefited from foreign investment.

Bende-Nabende et al. (2001) studied the impact of FDI through spillover effects on economic growth of the ASEAN-5 for the period of 1970-1996. They found that FDI accelerates economic growth either directly or through spillover effects. They showed that the impact of FDI on economic growth is positive and significant for Indonesia, Malaysia, and Philippines, while they identify a negative relationship for Singapore and Thailand. Furthermore, Bende-Nabende et al. (2003) show that the relationship between FDI and growth suffers from a strong endogeneity. Indeed, FDI first promotes growth, which is followed by a stable and rapid growth that can be a positive sign of attractiveness for TNCs.

By examining the effect of FDI on growth in the primary, manufacturing, and services sectors, Alfaro (2003) discovered that the impacts of FDI vary significantly across sectors. Using cross-section regressions with 47 countries for the time period of 1980 to 1999, her findings suggest that FDI has an ambiguous effect on growth. Nevertheless, overall FDI in manufacturing has a positive effect on growth, while FDI in the primary sector tends to portray a negative effect on growth. As for FDI impact on services sectors, evidence is ambiguous.

Li and Liu (2005) focus on the link between FDI and growth by studying panel techniques and simultaneous equations on a panel of 84 countries (21 developed and 63 developing). They found positive effects of FDI on economic growth through its interaction with human capital in developing countries, but a negative effect of FDI on economic growth via its interaction with the technology gap. Moreover, Li and Liu (2005) found that the existence of a technological gap between developing countries and rich countries is likely to limit the positive effects of FDI.

Table 2: Mixed Effects of FDI on Growth

Author (Year)	Methodology	Findings
Bosworth and Collins (1999)	The authors used regression analysis on panel data loans for 58 developing countries during the period of 1978-1995.	The results indicated that FDI inflows had a positive effect on investment, but an insignificant negative effect on the saving rate.
Agosin and Mayer (2000)	They used regression analysis on panel data of a sample of 32 countries but for a longer period (1970-1996).	They found that an increase of FDI inflows increased investment in Asia, led to crowding out effects in Latin America and neutral effects in Africa.

Author (Year)	Methodology	Findings
Bende-Nabende et al. (2001.)	They studied the impact of FDI through spillover effects on economic growth of the ASEAN-5 for the period of 1970-1996.	The impact of FDI on economic growth is positive and significant for Indonesia, Malaysia, and Philippines, but negative for Singapore and Thailand.
Alfaro (2003)	She used cross-sectional regressions with 47 countries for the time period of 1980 to 1999.	FDI in manufacturing have positive effects on growth, but negative effects in the primary sector. For services sectors, evidences are ambiguous.
Li and Liu (2005)	They used panel techniques and simultaneous equations on a panel of 84 countries (21 developed and 63 developing).	They found positive effects of FDI on growth through its interaction with human capital in developing countries, but negative effects of FDI on growth via its interaction with the technology gap.

No Effects of FDI on Growth

By the same token, Kahaliq and Noy (2007) investigated the impacts of foreign direct investment (FDI) on economic growth using detailed sectorial data for FDI inflows to Indonesia over the period of 1997-

2006. At the aggregate level, FDI is observed to have a positive effect on economic growth. However, when accounting for the different average growth performance across sectors, the beneficial impact of FDI is no longer apparent. When examining different impacts across sectors, estimation results show that the composition of FDI matters for its effect on economic growth, with very few sectors showing positive impact of FDI and one sector even showing a robust negative impact of FDI inflows (mining and quarrying).

Similar, to the results from empirical studies on the impacts of FDI on economic growth, it appears that the relationship between FDI and growth is ambiguous. Mixed results underlie the idea that the effects of FDI heavily depend on the characteristics of the host country and the nature of FDI in question. A more favorable effect of FDI on a host economy is closely related to the spread of externalities or spillovers to local firms by multinationals. Such externalities may not take place because of weak linkages with local firms or low absorption capacity of host countries (Kumar and Pradhan, 2002).

Brewer and Young (2000) argue in the same direction that the impact of FDI on growth will therefore depend on the type of FDI, the structures of the host countries and the interactions that may or may not develop between the variables such as human capital, domestic investment, foreign trade, etc

Table 3: No Effects of FDI on Growth

Author (Year)	Methodology	Findings
Kholdy (1995)	Granger causality tests, using data from 10 East Asian economies.	The author did not find a causative link between FDI and productivity.
Carkovic and Levine (2002)	They analyzed a data sample of a panel of 72 countries, ranging from the United States to Rwanda.	The results of their analyses show that exogenous components of FDI have no effect on growth.
Nair-Reichert and Weinhold (2001)	They used the Holtz-Eakin causality test on a panel of 24 developing countries between 1971 and 1995.	They found no causal relationship between FDI and growth.
Katerina et al. (2004)	They investigated the existence and the nature of the effect of FDI on the rate of growth of a panel of 17 transition economies.	Their results indicate that FDI does not exhibit any significant relationship with economic growth in transition countries.

Much like theoretical literature, empirical literature has not reached a consensus on the impact of FDI on economic growth. Accordingly, we may find arguments that suggest both positive and negative effects of FDI on economic growth. Therefore, results are mixed. These contradictory findings may be due to a number of methodological and conceptual factors, including the lack of comprehensive harmonized data, various definitions of FDI, growth, and different econometric specifications.

Beyond economic and methodological reasons set forth above that can explain the mixed results of the effect of FDI on economic growth, several technical critiques can be formulated with respect to different empirical studies. Indeed, several studies on the FDI-growth relationship were performed in a static and comparative framework (panel and cross-sectional data) without taking into consideration the specificity of the countries studied in most case. Even when host countries were taken into account, the dynamic effect of FDI on growth was often neglected by researchers. The presence of spillovers implies an interaction between various determinants of growth, which makes it necessary to introduce this dynamic aspect in different analyze. Moreover, given that FDI could be attracted by countries with high rates of growth, observed relationships may suffer from causality issues.

Another problem results from the omission of important variables in explaining economic growth. Indeed, in several empirical studies, only one or two variables have been introduced aside from FDI to explain economic growth. This is hardly consistent with the study of a relationship between growth and FDI, as the omission of variables may lead to misleading estimates in which FDI could significantly be correlated to other variables, which in turn may affect growth. In this case, the omission of important variables in the regression equation may lead to biased estimations of the FDI coefficient, since it would most likely absorb the impact of these omitted variables. Thus, it becomes crucial to know in what ways and to what extent FDI interacts with other explanatory variables. Several factors are likely to have a positive impact on growth factors such as human capital, domestic capital formation, exchange, technology transfer, etc. However, while FDI promotes growth, it does not necessarily mean that it produces the same effect on reducing poverty.

Chapter 7

FDI, Growth, and Poverty

Most previous studies assume that economic growth and welfare are positively correlated and hence, use GDP growth as a proxy for welfare. However, this implicit postulation has been recently challenged (Anand and Sen 2000). Evidence shows that GDP growth can occur while poverty incidence is also increasing.

Indeed, the distribution of income is as important as the variation in the process of poverty reduction. In this sense, FDI can have leverage on the triangle growth-inequality-poverty. In the following subsections, we analyze mechanisms through which growth, inequality, and poverty interact.

Dollar and Kraay (2002) test the effect of growth and trade liberalization on poverty, distinguishing countries open to globalization from others. They found that trade openness and FDI promote distribution-neutral growth. As a result, this growth is somewhat beneficial for the poor. By the same token, Beck et al. (2004) studied the effects of financial development on growth, inequality, and poverty. They found that financial intermediation promotes income growth of the poor more than the rich, thus reducing inequality. However, Nissanke and Thorbecke (2006) find that globalization affects poverty in an inverse "U" process. Here, threshold effects play an important role. According to these authors, the agricultural development in poor countries is more important than trade and financial openness for the promotion of development. Under this assumption, FDI in the agricultural sector can play a significant role (Tsai, 1995).

Nevertheless, the reduction of poverty does not depend on economic growth alone. According to Bourguignon (2003), it also depends on simultaneous changes in the growth rate in median income and the distribution function. Thus, there are several hypotheses for the reduction of poverty. First, economic growth with neutral distributional effects is likely to increase both the income of the poor and the rest of the population. Then, a redistribution to reduce inequality, even constant middle income, is also likely to raise a portion of the population above the absolute poverty line. Finally, in extreme cases, the increase in inequality can offset the effects of growth on poverty reduction. This depends on the elasticity of income for poor populations with respect to growth and inequality. In this sense, structural and institutional characteristics of a country play a primary role.

As a result, two kinds of effects on poverty can be highlighted: a growth effect and an inequality effect. However, these two effects interact between them according to the development strategy adopted by the country, depending on the objectives, ideologies, and political orientations of the governments. The controversy about these strategies gave rise to the concept of pro-poor.

Pro-Poor Growth

The economic literature on development has been marked by the emergence of the concept of pro-poor growth (Kakwani and Pernia, 2000; Ravallion and Chen, 2003; Lopez, 2004; Klasen, 2004; Kraay, 2004; Ravallion, 2004; Kakwani and Son, 2008). Henceforth, it is not enough to stimulate growth but also to ensure that it is conducive to poverty reduction. To this end, there is a debate on the definition of "pro-poverty growth" that focuses on two main views.

In the first view, supported by Kakwani and Pernia (2000), pro-poor growth is a growth that changes the distribution of income in favor of the poorest quintile. Thus, the growth of incomes of the poor should be higher than that of the rich, which would result in a reduction of inequalities.

In the second view, growth is said to be pro-poor when it decreases the rate of absolute poverty, regardless of changes in dissimilarities between the different quintiles of the population (Ravallion, 2004). This approach to pro-poor growth is highly dependent on the chosen measure of poverty. Indeed, it is valid only to determine the absolute poverty line (see definition of poverty).

These two approaches offer competing outlooks of pro-poor growth. In the first approach, growth should reduce poverty while lowering inequality. In the second approach, growth should reduce poverty regardless of inequalities. Thus, it is clear that the dilemma between the two visions concerns the determination of the role of inequality.

FDI and Inequality

The role of FDI in the growth-inequality-poverty is crucial. Indeed, the effects of FDI on poverty not only depend on their effects on growth, but also on their distribution factors. The model of Heckscher-Ohlin-Samuelson (H.O.S) shows that FDI and trade openness are likely to increase inequality between sectors with a comparative advantage and other sectors. When there is a high level of inequality, the level of poverty is likely to remain insensitive to FDI induced growth. The structure of poor populations may be affected so as to have more labor sectors that lack comparative advantages.

The effects of FDI on inequalities can be analyzed according to the hypothesis of dependency theories developed by Amin and Prebisch. In this case, FDI leads to the marginalization of peripheral countries while promoting the formation of an elite class that benefit from expanding sectors. However, unlike in the Kuznets model, dependency theories show that economic and political elites have an incentive to maintain a high level of inequality to protect their acquisitions. Here, FDI would lead to a continued increase in inequality within countries.

Empirically speaking, Tsai (1995) examined the change in the GINI coefficient as a function of economic growth, FDI inflows, and other political and geographic instrumental variables. He found that FDI increase income inequalities especially in Asian countries, although the effect is marginal and depends on geographic considerations. Nevertheless, Tsai's study (1995) showed that the economic development level, public consumption and the improvement of the agricultural sector are crucial to understand the level of inequality. Likewise, Choi (2006) used recent World Bank data on inequalities to test the effect of FDI stocks inflows and outflows on the GINI coefficient. The author found that FDI inflows and outflows increase inequality.

Chapter 8

Gender Parity through TNCs

Female represent the majority of people affected by poverty in developing countries. Therefore, it is very interesting to wonder about the mechanisms that link multinational corporations and poverty reduction as it relates to female..

Much of the studies on the gender effects of FDI focus on specific case studies and are limited by the lack of gender-specific data, or by the difficulty of disentangling the impacts of FDI from the impacts of other simultaneous transformations. Most of the time, it is difficult to demonstrate FDI benefits for women. However, the main body of evidence suggests a positive effect, even though some papers have shown the opposite; there is still more to learn.

Significant literatures reviewed in this study analyze the impacts of FDI on women employment and income, in absolute terms and relative to men. Few studies analyze the effects of such reforms on education opportunities, health, and the general wellbeing of women. In the following pages, we will briefly comment on mechanisms through which FDI affects gender inequality.

Transnational corporations implantation through FDI alters domestic prices, including wages, adjusting production, the use of inputs and the distribution of income between the different resources. Indeed, FDI may affect differently the employment and wages of different social groups, skilled and unskilled workers, as well as women and men. In the same way, FDI may also reshape relative employment and wages of such different groups.

The main mechanism through which FDI operates consists on changes in the relative prices of goods. Switching relative prices of goods modifies economic agents' incentives; induces the reallocation of production factors and modifies their relative use. Changes in the relative prices of goods may also differently affect the consumption and income of different groups, such as men and women, depending on preferences and expenditure restrictions. In the case of labor, FDI modifies employment and wages of different groups, including women and men. Moreover, reductions on government revenues due to the decrease of tariffs and quotas may affect different groups differently as a consequence of changes on government expenditure and reallocation of public resources.

Becker´s theory (1957) states that increased competition in the product market will reduce discrimination against women and minorities in the long run. According to this view, higher wages and better employment opportunities brought by FDI will force local competition to react, modifying relative prices, especially for inputs, hence, affecting different groups. Multinational corporations may also change individual preferences in host countries, bringing new ways of seeing employment and labor rights, and reducing discrimination (Black and Brainerd, 2004).

The impacts of FDI on gender disparity depend on global and local conditions such as public institutions, consumer habits, resource endowments and labor market. However, if FDI give a boost to economic growth, which will improves the quality of public services, gender disparities in human capital, such as health and education, will tend to fall (Aguayo, 2011).

Another channel through which FDI can affect gender disparity is through technology transfers. International competition through FDI can lead to the adoption of more capital and skill-intensive technologies. These technologies may be more complementary with female labor, increasing the relative demand of women and therefore their relative employment and wages (Arnold and Javorik, 2009; Galor and Weil, 1996; Welch, 2000).

Chapter 9

Supply of Infrastructure through TNCs

FDI can affect poverty through other mechanisms including the supply of certain TNCs oriented toward provision of resources for the population likely to reduce exclusion and deprivation. In this sense, the provision of infrastructure for access to water, energy, health care and transportation can improve the lives of the poorest.

An essential requirement for economic growth and sustainable development in developing countries is the provision of efficient, consistent, and inexpensive infrastructure services, such as water and sanitation, electrical power, transport and telecommunications. The availability of efficient infrastructure services is an important determinant of the market development pace and output growth, along with access to affordable infrastructure services for consumption purposes serves to improve household welfare, especially among the poor. In most countries, however, the potential contribution of infrastructure to economic growth and poverty reduction has not been fully realized, and existing infrastructure stock and services fall far short of the requirements (Kirkpatrick et al., 2006).

Traditionally, infrastructure was the exclusive province of the public sector. Since the mid-1980s, governments of the vast majority of countries around the world have pursued policies to involve the private sector in the delivery and financing of infrastructure services. Privatization was thought to promote more efficient operations, expand service delivery, reduce the financial burden on government and increase the level of foreign and domestic private investment (World Bank, 1995). Early privatization measures focused on the manufacturing sector. However, in recent years, the private sector has become more and more involved in the financing and delivery of infrastructure services. A large number of developing countries have introduced private participation into their infrastructure industries and, by the end of 2001, developing countries had received over $755 billion in private investment flows in nearly 2,500 infrastructure projects (World Bank, 2003).

Utilities such as water supply, gas, electricity, telecommunication, and certain modes of transportation all have had natural monopoly characteristics arising from pervasive economies of scale and scope. Since the 1990s, a significant part of the increase in FDI in the services sector has been the growth in private capital flows for infrastructure in response to the general trend towards privatization of infrastructure in developing countries.

On the contrary, during the 1990s, aggregate flows of official development assistance for infrastructure projects fell by half during the course of the decade (Willoughby, 2002). Participation of the private sector in the provision of infrastructure services began in the early 1990s in a few pioneer countries, including Argentina, Chile, Malaysia, and Mexico. Since 1990, Private Participation in Infrastructure (PPI) projects in developing countries has risen dramatically and spread throughout the developing world: more than 137 developing countries have implemented infrastructure projects with private participation in at least one sector since 1990 (World Bank, 2010). According to the World Bank's Private Participation in Infrastructure database, the annual investment commitments reached a peak of $128 billion in 1997. Between 1984 and 2005, 150 low and middle income countries transferred the operating risk for 3,268 infrastructure projects attracting investment commitments of $962 billion.

Chapter 10

Socially Responsible Investing

It is difficult to define socially responsible investing (SRI), since it is a polysemous concept that has been the subject of lengthy debates. Socially responsible investing has Judeo-Christian roots with scholars tracing the earliest form of social screening of investment opportunities to the Hebrew Bible back over two thousand years (Ciocchetti, 2007). John Wesley, the founder of Methodism, in his sermon titled "The Use of Money," proclaimed that good Christians should "gain all [they] can without hurting [their] neighbor" (Jackson, 1872). Thus, Methodists, followed by the Quakers and others, developed the habit of refusing to support companies involved with alcohol, gambling, or tobacco.

From the seventeenth century until the mid-twentieth century, the concept of socially-screened investment remained a small religiously-centered movement. In the 1960s, investors took a renewed interest in socially responsible investing when civil rights movement, embodied by Martin Luther King, movements against the Vietnam War, women's rights, and environmental movements emerged. Key issues for SRI advocated in the 1970s were the nuclear arms race and the environment. It was during the 1970s that the first socially responsible mutual funds were created allowing investors to pool their funds together to achieve greater social returns. In the 1980s, world-wide public attention was focused on apartheid in South Africa and companies were lobbied by the SRI community – and eventually mandated by the Anti- Apartheid Act of 1986

– to stop doing business in South Africa (Arjalies, 2010; Ciocchetti, 2007).

Socially Responsible Investment (SRI) is an economic and social phenomenon that has led to a growing interest of both academics and professionals for several years. Investment style booming, particularly favored by the emergence of the concept of sustainable development, is to integrate SRI in the investment process of extra-financial criteria supposed to reveal the corporate social responsibility (Arjalies, 2010).

The Social Investment Forum (SIF)[6] defines socially responsible investing (SRI) as "an investment process that considers social and environmental consequences of investments, both positive and negative, within the context of rigorous financial analysis." In simple terms, SRI is generally considered to be the act of consistently investing in companies that are believed to have a positive impact on society, and/or avoiding companies that affect society in negative ways.

According to Ciocchetti (2007), "Socially responsible investing" (SRI) refers to financial

---

6. -The Social Investment Forum is a non-profit organization based in the United States, working for the promotion and growth of socially responsible investing. It has over 400 members, including investment management and advisory firms, mutual fund companies, banks, non-profit organizations and other members of the investment community.

contributions into investment vehicles designed to combine the traditional investment philosophy favoring profit-maximization with a values-based component seeking non-financial benefits. Such non-financial benefits are often referred to as social returns. These social returns vary in scope, but can be broadly defined as company policies and actions that enhance a socially responsible investor's specific environmental, religious, or social values. These enhancements may or may not have any impact on the profit-maximization component of the socially responsible investment and may actually cause a socially responsible investment to decrease in value. Socially responsible investing is the common term for this practice in the United States but the concept is also referred to as "ethical investing," primarily in the United Kingdom, or "values-based investing."

Today, major TNCs are entering the realm of socially responsible investing. According to the 2010 Trends report of Social Investment Forum (SIF) – the most prominent SRI industry group – over $3.07 trillion was invested in 2009 in professionally managed portfolios that implemented at least one core aspect of socially responsible investing. New guidelines for TNCs in socially responsible investment (SRI) and sustainable development certainly have undeniable effects on the poor in host countries.

Socially responsible investing is usually divided into three categories: (1) social screening (2) shareholder advocacy and (3) community investing. These three categories are not mutually exclusive; indeed, a socially responsible investor may practice social screening while also investing in community development projects. The majority of socially responsible investors, however, focus on social screening and shareholder advocacy although community investing is growing in prominence as the SRI movement itself expands.

The following categories of socially responsible investing, described by Ciocchetti (2007) in the Encyclopedia of Business Ethics and Society, have been identified based on an assessment of public water supply and sanitation systems (Idelovitch and Ringskog 1995).

Social Screening

The basic premise underlying social screening is the idea that companies that meet social standards required by SRI screens will be the most profitable and successful companies in the long-term. Social screening is a means by which investors either invest in a particular company based on the company's social record – or lack thereof, or divest a financial holding.

Shareholder Advocacy

Investors desiring to change corporate practices frequently turn to the shareholder advocacy category. Shareholder advocacy proponents attempt to take advantage of share ownership and the potential of such ownership to obtain access to management and to other shareholders. While social screening is intended to serve the dual purpose of altering the supply and demand equation for a specific company stock and to satisfy the ethical desires of the socially responsible investor, this category is not the only mean at the disposal of socially responsible investors to satisfy their goals.

Community Investment

The goal of community investing is to offer access to basic banking services, capital, credit, equity and healthcare previously unavailable inside the community. Community investment is the process by which socially responsible investors directly invest funds into lower-income and less economically successful communities which have been historically underserved by traditional financial services. These programs are designed to encourage economic growth such areas desperately in need. Community development capital is most often used in micro-lending initiatives to lower-income entrepreneurs, building affordable housing and assisting in employment efforts within the immediate area. Community Development Financial Institutions (CDFIs) – such as specialized banks and credit unions, venture capital community development accounts and micro-enterprise loan funds– receive the majority of these funds and serve as the distribution center for the community investment area.

It might be noticed that the socially responsible investing categories listed above are applied at varying levels to other public services, such as electrical power, telephone, and transport.

Chapter 11

Strategies to enhance the contribution of TNCs on poverty reduction

Findings of theoretical and empirical studies on the impact of TNCs on poverty show that there are no universal answers to the question: How can TNCs contribute to poverty reduction in a host country? However, there is an agreement on the fact that TNCs have the potential of financing poverty reduction under certain conditions.

The question is: how can the effectiveness of the financing of poverty reduction by multinational enterprises be ensured? To reduce poverty through TNC financing, certain requirements and sufficient conditions must be fulfilled. To do so, a prolonged agenda must be set up. In the following pages, we set out strategies that might improve the contribution of TNCs on poverty reduction.

Improving Governance of Local Institutions

The importance of institutions and investment climate is a major requirement in the process of economic growth and poverty reduction. Both factors refer to good governance in three dimensions[7]: political, economic, and administrative.

According to many experts, the economic performance of a country primarily depends on good governance (OECD, 2001). In this view, there is a

7. - The World Bank identified three distinct dimensions or aspects of governance:(a) the form of the political regime; (b) the process by which authority is exercised in the management of a country's economic and social resources for development; and (c) the capacity of governments to design, formulate, and implement policies and discharge functions.

positive relationship between good governance, economic growth, and poverty reduction. Far from being a mere slogan, good governance is imperative for countries that are determined to ensure their economic growth and reduce poverty level. Indeed, good governance plays a key role in the attraction of foreign capital, in the distribution of national income and in the process of poverty reduction. The economic literature reveals that there is a strong relationship between institutional quality, economic growth, and poverty level. To effectively ensure good governance of local institutions in TNCs' host countries, improving human capital through various education and training is fundamental.

To do so, available local human capital should be educated in at least 3 different ways. First, active human capital in TNCs host countries must be educated and trained to practice good governance through effective application of punitive or rewarding sanctions according to the law. Indeed, given the high rate of corruption and fraud in countries where poverty reigns, improvement of human capital is not only based on knowledge or learned skills. Human capital employed in these countries will actually improve if punitive sanctions are applied to curb corruption and mismanagement as well as rewarding sanctions to promote good management.

> The mentality of men (and women) is like a liquid that takes the shape of the container in which it is placed. People that live in an environment that advocates, encourages and rewards those who steal, corrupt and mismanage, will adopt unproductive attitudes and behaviors quickly. In contrast, people who live in an environment where theft, corruption, mismanagement and crime are punished and, where rewards are given to those who make the effort to work without compromise, people will end up adopting constructive and productive mentalities and practices in a very short time.[8]

In order to improve human capital and promote good governance, local governments and other organizations should organize professional training and internships in host countries in which TNCs operate. This is to fill the gaps or deficiencies in active human capital in local institutions, promote adaptation to

---

8. Interview Exclusive of Eric Mulumba Zozo in Adunagow Magazine Issue 19, Jan/Feb 2011

change, and raise human capital productivity level. Training and continuing education for adults should be organized to enhance and expand the skills of those who have not completed extensive studies. This does not mean that the recruitment of human capital in local host countries institutions should be completed without meeting any standards. Rather, recruiting should be based on proven skills to ensure further human capital performance.

Finally, for good governance to be durable, particular attention must be paid to the formal educational system, from elementary school to higher education. Formal education defined as a set of regular teachings provided in elementary, secondary and tertiary institutions, and acknowledged by a certificate or a diploma, remains the foundation of the educational system. Therefore, local governments, international development agencies, Non-Governmental Organizations (NGOs) and TCNs must invest in promoting an educational system that is accessible to all levels of the population and adapted to local needs in primary, secondary, and tertiary sectors.

Encouraging TNCs to Be More Involved in Reducing Poverty Level

TNCs are not intended to create a reliable institutional, economic or social framework and their mission is not to ensure an equitable distribution of income. The purpose of TNCs is to generate and maximize profit. However, it is important to note that the purpose that drives TNCs to seek profit is not inconsistent with the process of economic growth, sustainable development, and poverty reduction. The point is to find a common ground to allow different parties to benefit.

The persistence of poverty puts TNCs at a future risk position, especially in developing countries but also in developed countries. Poverty can compromise the existence and expansion of TNCs around the world. In fact, people who suffer because of poverty or lack of essential resources supported by others are predisposed to react with violence by promoting different kinds of troubles. Global poverty can favor unpredictable social tensions in TNCs' host countries. A single strike can turn into sabotages, boycotts, lootings, profound crises and civil wars consequently destroying TNC activities and profits.

By not doing enough to promote the welfare of its workers and local communities, TNCs are jeopardizing their future. In fact, by weakening their workers and local communities where they do business, TNCs may, in the long run, compromise their own sustainability. TNCs should continuously make efforts to do good to people in places where they operate and they should avoid harming their workers as well as communities with which they interact. This implies that TNCs may provide good salaries, good work conditions for their employees and promote social development of local communities in which they are established. As Stiglitz (2007:198) said:

> "Doing good can be good for business, and doing bad can subject companies to expensive lawsuits. Bad behavior also can harm a company's image: the negative publicity surrounding the U.S. shoe company Nike after its suppliers in Vietnam mistreated local workers and the furor after Ken Saro-Wiwa was killed in Nigeria amid accusations that Anglo-Dutch oil company Shell supported the military junta that murdered him

were wake-up calls. Executives realized that they could be blamed for problems thousands of miles away from headquarters. Events like these have led to a number of voluntary initiatives by companies to improve the lot of their workers and the communities where they do business."

International development agencies, local governments, local communities[9] and Non-Governmental Organizations must make more efforts to convince TNCs about the merits of their involvement in reducing poverty level. Indeed, increasing TNCs involvement in poverty reduction will help multinational firms not just avoid social tensions and negative publicity images, but it will also help them expand their activities, to gain more consumers and to benefit from the higher quality of their labor forces. Thus, to be effective, TNCs must not only speak in favor of poverty reduction but act accordingly with consistency.

---

9. Local community is a group of interacting people living in a common location, organized around common values and attributed with social cohesion. Local communities vary in size, composition, structure, and organization and include local government authorities, as well as the local businesses, schools, and cultural activities.

Establishing a Close collaboration between TNCs, NGOs and Local Communities

It is a fact that TNCs are meant to pursue profit and therefore often do not necessarily have the ability to implement philanthropic projects to fight against poverty. Additionally, a great number of TNCs that have established organizations and philanthropic projects to reduce poverty are often not effective in the social sector. Furthermore, their actions have been accused of subtly preserving their markets and profits.

However, there are a large number of NGOs designed to fight against poverty with their experience and expertise to ensure the implementation of projects aiming to reduce poverty level. These NGOs seldom receive enough financial resources to ensure the sustainability of their projects. Often NGOs receive periodic or episodic non-renewable funding. This limits them in their actions. The ability to obtain additional financing from TNCs wishing to fight against poverty would be likely to increase the effectiveness for NGOs that can effectively contribute to the substantial reduction of poverty.

Moreover, despite the recommendations of many experts and international development agencies to promote a participatory approach[10], local communities are still often excluded in the design of projects against poverty. It is proven that no project against poverty can succeed if local communities benefiting from these projects are not involved in their design and implementation. Indeed, local populations are well positioned to effectively contribute to the identification of their needs, the design of strategies and the implementation of solutions. Indeed, the sustainability of a project is only possible when the project beneficiaries take ownership.

It should be noted that a local community can be effective in the design and implementation of projects that reduce poverty if it is coordinated and represented by representatives of the various segments of the local population. Indeed, if for example, representatives of local communities mainly belong to the elite, they will tend to promote the implementation of projects for the elite to the detriment of other layers of the population

---

10. The concept of participatory approach is a method in which people or local communities called 'beneficiaries' have a role in the process of design and implementation of development activities

who are much poorer. Also, it should be ensured that representatives and local community leaders are willing, able and determined to stay in the region and not to emigrate thereafter. This is to avoid breaking the cycle and affect the sustainability of implemented projects.

The establishment of a close collaboration between TNCs, NGOs, local communities and international agencies would allow TNCs to fund consistent projects jointly designed with experienced NGOs, local communities and international agencies of development. The choices and design of projects initiated by experienced NGOs and local communities in collaboration with international agencies of development and TNCs will favor a better implementation and effectiveness of projects. A close collaboration of those key actors will surely increase chances of poverty reduction projects to succeed.

To facilitate collaboration between NGOs, TNCs, International development agencies and local communities and to assure its effectiveness, it is necessary to establish local frameworks which can be named Local Development Frames (LDFs). LDFs will be constituted by representatives of TNCs, experienced

NGOs, local communities, and International development agencies. LDFs would target people and areas that have recurrent needs, possibilities for projects to reduce poverty and elaborate requirements for the selection of projects likely to be financed by TNCs. These projects will have the merit of both meeting persistent needs of poor that have been left behind and promote the progress of TNCs and local communities in an atmosphere of peace and harmony.

Project funding will be implemented in different ways. First, NGOs in association with local communities will be able to implement some projects and submit them through LDFs to solicit request funding from TNCs. Second, TNCs could call for projects aiming to finance activities led by NGOs and local communities to respond to local needs. Projects will be analyzed and approved by an ad hoc commission established by LDFs. Approved or selected projects will be financed by funds made available by TNCs.

To ensure an optimal implementation of projects financed by transnational corporations, a follow-up in the execution of projects will necessarily have to be ensured by a team of assessors. This team of assessors will have to be representative in order to take into account the requirements of all LDFs components involved in the conception, financing and execution of the selected projects.

CONCLUSION

The review of empirical and theoretical literature on the contribution of TNCs through FDI to poverty reduction reveals that TNCs have the potential to reduce poverty in developing countries under certain conditions. However, there are no unanimous results of prior studies on institutional and economic mechanisms of FDI effects on poverty. Studies of institutional and economic mechanisms suggest both positive and perverse FDI effects on poverty reduction.

Prior research on institutional mechanisms of FDI effects on poverty reveals that FDI can have a positive or negative impact on local institutions and can affect the redistribution of income. By using their position to encourage the state to make necessary administrative reforms to facilitate economic transactions, TNCs may enhance the regularization of local institutions. In contrast, FDI can create distortions in local institutions when revenues from foreign trade or FDI fall into the host countries leader hands. Furthermore, studies on institutional mechanism reveal that good governance promotes beneficial allocation of income to poor people, while bad governance favors redistribution that increases the level of inequality and poverty.

The study of economic mechanisms of FDI effects on poverty addresses mixed effects of two approaches, including direct and indirect FDI impacts on poverty.

The microeconomic approach that studies the direct effects of FDI on poverty demonstrates that the entry of TNCs in an economy can create jobs and generate stimulatory effects or crowd out local firms. To be efficient, job creation should be more important than job destruction due to crowd out of local firms due to the entry of TNCs. The literature mentions that FDI effects on poverty do not only work if the employment rate alone increase; but the quality and location of employment must also be taken into consideration.

The macroeconomic approach studies the indirect effects of FDI on poverty through economic growth in three different ways. First, FDI can affect growth and poverty reduction through capital stock expansion in host countries. Second, the allocation of tax revenue collected from foreign firms can promote growth. Third, FDI can contribute to economic growth and poverty reduction through the transfer of new technologies, knowledge, and other intangible assets.

Several research studies have been devoted to the causality direction between FDI and economic growth using a number of econometric techniques. Findings from these studies are mixed and can be grouped into three categories. The first group of studies reports that FDI does increase growth. The second group of studies suggests negative effects of FDI on growth. The last group of studies establishes both positive and negative effects of FDI on economic growth. Nevertheless, while

FDIs do promote growth, it does not necessarily mean that it produces the same effect on reducing poverty.

FDIs can affect poverty through other mechanisms including the supply of infrastructures and socially responsible investments. As a matter of fact, FDI provides provision of infrastructure for access to water, energy, health care and transportation that can improve the lives of the poorest, reduce exclusion and deprivation. Furthermore, FDIs based on socially responsible investing (SRI) concept which is a process that considers social and environmental consequences of investments, can promote sustainable development and reduce global poverty.

Despite the fact that findings of studies of FDI's impact on poverty are mixed, there is an agreement that TNCs have the potential of financing poverty reduction under certain conditions. To reduce global poverty we proposed strategies that can be used to better capture or enhance TNC's contribution on poverty reduction.

To establish good governance of host country institutions, improvement of human capital through various education and training is crucial. Human capital in TNCs host countries should be educated in at least 3 different ways. Active human capital in TNCs host countries must be educated and trained to practice good governance by effective application of punitive or rewarding sanctions according to the law. Training and continuing education should be organized to enhance and expand the skills of human capital assets in host countries. Governments, international development agencies, NGOs, and TNCs must invest in promoting the formal educational system that is accessible to all levels of the population and adapted to local needs in all sectors.

International development agencies, local governments, local communities and NGOs efforts must be made to convince TNCs about the merits of their involvement in reducing poverty. By not doing enough to promote the welfare of its workers and local communities, TNCs are jeopardizing their future. Undeniably, increasing TNCs involvement in poverty reduction will help multinational corporations not just avoid social pressures and negative publicity, but it will also help them to expand their activities and gain more.

The establishment of a close collaboration between TNCs, NGOs, local communities and international agencies would allow TNCs to fund consistent projects jointly designed with experienced NGOs, local communities and international development agencies. To facilitate and ensure effective collaboration between those key actors, it is necessary to establish Local Development Frames (LDFs). LDFs constituted by local communities' representatives would target people and areas that have recurrent needs and elaborate criteria for approbation of TNCs financing projects. NGOs with local communities will have opportunity to submit proposals to request TNCs financings through LDFs. Besides, TNCs will address calls projects aiming to finance actions led by NGOs and Local Communities to finance projects that respond to local needs listed by LDFs.

The persistence of global poverty is great challenge that we must face with all available resources. Reducing poverty through TNCs is a truly inspiring and practical approach. In this book, we have demonstrated that TNCs have potentials to significantly contribute to economic growth and poverty reduction under certain conditions. We must get international agencies, TNCs, NGOs, local governments and communities involved in the process of poverty alleviation through appropriate strategies proposed in this book.

CONTENTS

REFERENCES

Aaron, C. (1999) The contribution of FDI to poverty alleviation. FIAS.

Acemoglu, D, Autor, D and Lyle, D (2004) "Women, War, and Wages: The Effect of Female Labor Supply on the Wage Structure at Midcentury", Journal of Political Economy, v.112, iss. 3, pp. 495-551.

Acemoglu, D., Johnson, S. and Robinson J. A. (2001) "The Colonial Origins of Comparative Development: An Empirical Investigation." American Economic Review 91(5): 1369-1401.

Acemoglu, D., Johnson, S. and Robinson J. A. (2005) "Institutions as the Fundamental Cause of Long Run Growth." NBER Working Paper 10481.

Acemoglu, D. and Robinson, J. A. (2008) Persistence of Power, Elites, and Institutions, .American Economic Review, 98, 267 293.

Agenor, P-R. (2004) Does Globalization Hurt the Poor? Journal of International Economics and Economic Policy 1(1), 21-51.

Agosin, M. R.and Mayer R. (2000) "Foreign Investment in Developing Countries. Does it Crowd in Domestic Investment?" UNCTAD/OSG/DP 146.

Aguayo-Téllez, E. (2011) The Impact of Trade Liberalization Policies and FDI on Gender Inequality: A Literature Review, World Bank Background paper for the World Development Report 2012, World Bank, Washington DC.

Ahluwalia, M. S., Carter, N. G. and Chenery, H.B. (1979) "Growth & Poverty in Developing Countries." Journal of Development Economics 6: 299-341.

Anand, S. and Sen, A. K. (2000) "Human Development and Economic Sustainability", World Development, Vol.28, No.12, 2029-49.

Aitken, B. J.and Harrison, A. E. (1999) "Do Domestic Firms Benefit from Direct Foreign Investment? Evidence from Venezuela." American Economic Review 89: 605-618.

Akyuz, Y. and Gore, C. (2001) "African Economic Development in a Comparative Perspective." Cambridge Journal of Economics 25: 268-288.

Alfaro, L., (2003) Foreign Direct Investment and Growth: Does the Sector Matter? Working Paper, Harvard Business School

Alfaro, L., Chanda, A., Kalemli-Ozcan, S. and Sayek, S. (2004) "FDI and economic growth: the role of local financial markets." Journal of International Economic 64: 89-112.

Alfaro, L. and Charlton, A. (2007) Growth and the Quality of Foreign Direct Investment: Is All FDI Equal?', Harvard Business School Working Paper 07-072.

Arjalies, D. L. (2010) « Qu'est-ce que l'Investissement Socialement Responsable ? » CNRS

Arnold, Jens M. and Beata Javorcik (2009), "Gifted Kids or Pushy Parents? Foreign Direct Investment and Plant Productivity in Indonesia," Journal of International Economics, forthcoming.

Apergis, N., Filippidis, I. and Economidou, C. (2007) "Financial Deeping and Economic Growth Linkages: A Panel Data Analysis" *Review of World Economics* 143, pp. 179-198.

Artadi, E. V. and Sala-i-Martin, X. (2003) «The Economic Tragedy of the XXth Century: Growth in Africa.» Harvard University and Columbia University.

Asiedu, E., (2001). "On the determinants of foreign direct investment to developing countries: Is Africa different?", World Development, vol. 30 n°1, p.107-119.

Asiedu, E., (2003) Foreign direct Investment to Africa: the role of Government Policy, Governance and Political Instability, Kansas : University of Kansas.

Asiedu, E. (2006) «Foreign Direct Investment in Africa: The Role of Natural Resources, Market Size, Government Policy,

Institutions & Political Instability.» The World Economy, 29(1), 63—77.

Atkinson, A. B. (1998) Poverty in Europe. Oxford, Blackwell.

Autor, D. and Katz, L. (1999) "Changes in the Wage Structure and Earnings Inequality," Ashenfelter, Orley; Card, David, eds. Handbook of Labor Economics, Volume 3A New York: North-Holland.

Bailey, D.H. (1989) "The Effects of Corruption in a Developing

Nation", Western Political Quarterly, vol. 19 n°4, p.719-732, 1966. Reprint in *Political Corruption: A Handbook*, A.J. Heidenheimer,

M. Johnston and V.T. LeVine (eds.), Oxford, Transaction Books, p.934- 952.

Balasubramanyam, V., Salisu, M. and Sapsford, D. (1996) "FDI and Growth in EP and IS Countries," *The Economic Journal* 106(434), 92-105.

Baldwin, R., H. Baraconier, and Forslid, R. (2005) «Multinationals, Endogenous Growth, and Technological Spillovers: Theory and Evidence.» Review of International Economics 13(5): 945-963.

Baliamoune-Lutz, Mina (2007) "Globalisation and Gender Inequality: Is Africa Different?", Journal of African Economies, v. 16, iss. 2, pp. 301-48.

Baltagi, B. H., Egger, P. and Pfaffermayr, M. (2007) «Estimating Models of Complex FDI: Are there third country effects» Journal of Econometrics 140(1): 260-281.

Baltagi, B. H., Egger, P. and Pfaffermayr, M. (2008) «Estimating regional trade agreement effects on FDI in an interdependent world» Journal of Econometrics 145: 194-208.

Barrios, S., Gorg, H. and Strobl, E. (2005) «Foreign Direct Investment, Competition & Industrial Development in the host country.» European Economic Review 49: 1761-1784.

Barro, R. J. and Lee, J.-W. (2001) «International Data on educational attainment: updates and implications.» Oxford Economic Papers 53: 541-563.

Bastos, F. and Nasir J. (2004) «Productivity & the Investment

Climate: What Matters Most?» World Bank Policy Research WP N° 3335.

Beck, T. Demirguc-kunt and Levine (2004) "Finance, Inequality, and Poverty: Cross Country Evidence" NBER Working Paper,

W10979. 423

Becker, Gary (1957) "The Economics of Discrimination," Chicago: The University of Chicago Press.

Bende-Nabende, Ford, J.L, Slater, J.R (2000) 'The Impact of FDI and Regional Economic Integration on The Economic Growth of The ASEAN-5 Economies, 1970-1994 : A comparative Analysis in a small Structral Model', in Ford J.L (ed), Finance, Governance and Economic Performance in Pacific and South East Asia, Edwar Elgar.

Bende–Nabende, A., Ford, J. and Slater, J. (2001) "FDI, regional economic integration and endogenous growth: some evidence from Southeast Asia", *Pacific Economic Review*, 6 (3): 383–399.

Bende-Nabende, A., Ford, J., Santoso, B. and Sen S. (2003) «The interaction between FDI, output and the spillover variabes: cointegration and VAR analyses for APEC, 1965-1999» Applied Economics Letters 10(3): 165-172.

Bengoa, M. and Robles, S. (2003) FDI, Economic Freedom, and Growth: New Evidence from Latin America. *European Journal of Political Economy, 19*, 529-545.

Bienayme, A. (1998) *Principes de concurrence*.

Black, Sandra E. and Brainerd, Elizabeth (2004) "Importing Equality? The Impact of Globalization on Gender Discrimination", Industrial and Labor Relations Review, v. 57, iss. 4, pp. 540-59.

Blomstrom, M. and Kokko, A. (1996) «The Impact of Foreign Direct Investment on Host Countries: A Review of The Empirical Evidence» National Bureau of Economic Research.

Blomstrom, M., Kokko, A. and Zejan, M. (2000) *Foreign Direct Investment. Firm and Host Country Strategies*, London: Macmillan.

Borensztein, E., De Gregorio, J. and Lee, J-W. (1998) «How does foreign direct investment affect economic growth» Journal of International Economics 45(1): 115-135.

Bosworth, S. and Collins, S. (1999)"Capital Flows to Developing Economies: Implications for Saving and Investment," Brookings Papers on Economic Activity: 0 (1), pp. 143-69.

Bourdet, Y. and Falck, H. (2006) «Emigrants' remittances and Dutch Disease in Cape Verde» International Economic Journal **20**(3): 267- 284.

Bourguignon, F. (2002) «The Growth elasticity of Poverty reduction: Explaining heterogeneity across countries & time periods.

Bosworth, B. P. and Collins, S. M. (1999) «Capital inflows, investment, and growth « Tokyo Club Papers.

Bourguignon, F. (2003) The Poverty-Growth-Inequality Triangle. Indian Council for Research on International Economic Relations, New Delhy.

Braconier, H., Norback, P.-J. and Urban, D. (2002) «Vertical FDI Revisited.» Research Institute of Industrial Economics; Working Paper Series N° 579.

Brainard, L. (1997). «An Empirical Assessment of the Proximity- Concentration Trade-off Between Multinational Sales & Trade.

Brewer, T.L., Young L. (2000) *The Multinational Investment System and Multinational Enterprises*, Oxford University Press.

Butler, K.C. and Joaquin, D.C. (1998) “A note on political risk and the required return on foreign direct investment”, *Journal of International Business Studies*, vol. 29 n°3, p. 599-607.

Campos, N.F. and Kinoshita, Y. (2002) “FDI as technology transferred: some panel evidence from transition economies,” The Manchester School.

Carkovic, M. and Levine, R. (2002), “Does Foreign Direct Investment Accelerate Economic Growth?” http://www.worldbank.org/research/conferences/financial_globalization/fdi.pdf.

Chatterjee, S. and Mathur, R.D. (2003) Encouraging governance and transparency for investment, Global Forum on International Investment, Johannesburg (South Africa): OECD. http://www.oecd.org/dataoecd/26/7/19479227.pdf

Chen, S. and Ravaillon, M. (2008) «The Developing World is Poorer than We Thought, But No Less Successful in the Fight Against Poverty.» World Bank Policy Research Working Paper (N° 4703).

Chen, T.-J., Chen, H. and Ku Y. (2004) «Foreign Direct Investment & Local Linkage» Journal of International Business Studies 35: 320-333.

Chenery, H. and Strout, A. (1966) «Foreign assistance and economic development.» The American Economic Review 56(4): 679-733.

Choi C. (2006) Does foreign direct investment affect domestic income inequality? Applied Economics Letters, 13, 811-814.

Chudnovsky, D. and Lopez, A. (1999) Globalization and Developing Countries: Foreign Direct Investment and Growth and Sustainable Human Development, UNCTAD Occasional Paper.

Ciocchetti , C. A. (2007) «Socially Responsible Investing» *Encyclopedia of Business Ethics and Society*. Ed. Robert Kolb. Sage Publishing.

Collier, P. (2007). «Africa’s Economic Growth: Opportunity and Constraints» Centre for the Study of African Economies.

Collier, P. and Gunning, J. W. (1999) «Explaining African Economic Performance.» Journal of Economic Literature **37**: 64-111.

Corden, W.M. and Neary, J.P. (1982) «Booming Sector and Deindustrialisation in a Small Open Economy «. *The* Economic Journal 92 (December): 825-848.

De Mello, L.R. Jr. (1997) «Foreign Direct Investment in Developing Countries: A Selective Survey ,»Studies in Economics 9701, Department of Economics, University of Kent.

De Mello, L. R. Jr. (1999) «Foreign Direct Investment-Led Growth: Evidence from Time Series and Panel Data.» Oxford Economic papers, 1999, 51(1).

Dollar, D. (2004). «Globalization, Poverty & Inequality since 1980.» World Bank WP N° 3333.

Dollar, D and Gatti R (1999), "Gender Inequality, Income, and Growth: Are Good Time Good for Women?" World Bank Working Paper No. 1, Washington DC.

Dollar, D. and Kraay, A. (2002) «Growth is Good for the Poor» Journal of Economic Growth 7(3): 195-225.

Dollar, D., and Kraay, A. (2004) Trade, Growth, and Poverty. Economic Journal 114(493), F22-F49.

Duflo, Esther (2000), "Grandmothers and Granddaughters: Old Age Pension and IntraHousehold Allocation in South Africa", NBER Working Paper, No. 8061.

Dunning, J.H. (1977) "Trade, Location of Economic Activity and the MNE: A Search for an Eclectic Approach." In Bertil Ohlin, Per- Ove Hesselborn, and Per Magnus Wijkman, eds., The International Allocation of Economic Activity. London: Macmillan.

Dunning J. H. and Lundan, S. M. (2008) *Multinational Enterprises and the Global Economy*, Second edition, Great Britain.

Eifert, B., A. Gelb, and Ramachandran, V. (2008) «The Cost of

Doing Business in Africa: Evidence from Entreprise Survey Data»World Development(doi:10.1016/j.worlddev.2007.09.007).

Galor, Obed and Weil, David N (1996), "The Gender Gap, Fertility, and Growth", American Economic Review, v. 96, iss. 3, pp. 374-387.

Globerman, S. and Shapiro, D. (2002) "Global foreign direct investment flows: the role off governance infrastructure", World Development, vol. 30 n°11, p.1899-1919.

Gohou, G.,and Soumare, I. (2009) Impact of FDI on Poverty Reduction in Africa: Are there Regional Differences? African Economic Conference 11-13 November 2009,United Nations Conference Center, Addis Abeba.

Gorg, H. and Greenaway, D. (2003) «Much Ado About Nothing? Do Domestic Firms Really Benefit from Foreign Direct Investment?» IZA, Discussion Paper Series N° 944.

Grier, R. (2001). «Spillover effects of investment and education in Sub-saharan Africa.» University of Oklahoma.

Grossman, G. M., and Helpman, E. (1991) Innovation and growth in the global economy. MIT Press, Cambridge, Mass. and London.

Grossman, G. M., Helpman,E. and Szeidl, A.(2006) «Optimal integration strategies for the multinational firm.» Journal of International Economics 70(1): 216-238.

G8. (2005) Gleneagles summit [Accessed 14th March 2008]. http://www.g8summit.org/

Hayami, Y. (2001) Development Economics: From the Poverty to the Wealth of Nations. Oxford University Press.

Hanson, G. H., Mataloni, R.J., and Slaughter, M.J. (2001) «Expansion Strategies of U.S Multinational Firms.» National Bureau of Economic Research, Working Series WP N° 8433.

Harms, P. and Ursprung, H. W (2002) "Do Civil and Political

Repression Really Boost Foreign Direct Investments?", Economic Inquiry, vol. 40 n°4, p. 651-63.

Harrison, A. (Ed.). (2007). Globalization and Poverty. Chicago: The University of Chicago Press.

Hejazi, W. and P. Pauly (2003) «Motivations for FDI & Domestic Capital Formation» Journal of International Business Studies 34(3): 282-289.

Helpman, E. (1984). «A Simple Theory of International Trade with Multinational Corporations.» Journal of Political Economy 92(3).

Helpman, E., Melitz, M.J. and Yeaple, S. R. (2004) «Export versus FDI with Heterogeneous Firms.» The American Economic Review 94(1): 300-316.

Hansen, H. and Rand, J. (2006) On the causal links between FDI and growth in developing countries. *World Economy*, 29, 21-41.

Huntington, S.P. and Dominguez, J. I. (1975).“Political development”, in F.I. Greenstein and N.W. Polsby (eds.) Handbook of Political Science 3, Reading, Addison-Wesley, p.1-114.

Idelovitch, E. and Klas R. (1995) Private Sector Participation in water Supply and Sanitation in Latin America: Executive Summary, in Latin America: Executive Summary, URL: www.worldbank.org/html/lat/english/summary/ewsu/ps/water.htm.

Isham, J., Woolcock, M., Pritchett, L. and Busby, G. (2003) «The Varieties of Resource Experience: How Natural Resources Export Structures Affect the Political Economy of Economic Growth» Middlebury College Economics Discussion Paper N° 03-08.

Jackson, T. (1872) ”The Sermons of John Wesley. 50. The Use of Money - Luke 16:9”. Reprinted in 1999 by the Westley Center of Applied Theology. Northwest Nazarene University.

Javorcik, Beata (2004) “Does foreign Direct Investment Increase the Productivity of Domestic Firms? In Search of Spillovers through Backward Linkages”, American Economic Review, v. 94, iss. 3, pp. 605-627.

Jenkins, C. and Thomas, T. (2002) «Foreign Direct Investment in South Africa: Determinants, Characteristics and Implication for Economic Growh and Poverty Alleviation» Center for the Study of African Economies. University of Oxford.

Johnson, S., Ostry, J. D. and Subramanian, A. (2007) «The Prospects for Sustained Growth in Africa: Benchmarking the Constraints.» IMF Working Paper WP/07(52).

Kakwani, N. and Pernia, E. (2000) «What is Pro-poor Growth.» Asian Development Review 16: 1-22.

Kakwani, N. and Son, H. (2008) Poverty Equivalent Growth Rate, *Review of Income and Wealth*, 54, 643-655.

Khaliq, A., and Noy, I. (2007) Foreign direct Investment and economic growth: empirical evidence from sectoral data in Indonasia. *Journal of Economic Literature,* 45 (1), 313-325.

Katerina L, John P and Athanasios V (2004) Foreign Direct Investment and Economic Growth in Transition Economies. Sou East Eur J Eco 2(1): 97-110.

Kaufmann, D., Kraay A. and Zoido-Lobaton, P. (1999) "Governance Matters", World Bank, Working Paper n°2196.

Kholdy, S. (1995) Causality between foreign investment and spillover e ciency, *Applied Economics*, 27, 74-749.

Kirkpatrick, C., Parker, D. and Zhang, Y-F. (2006) "Foreign direct investment in infrastructure in developing countries: does regulation make a difference?" *Transnational Corporations,* Vol. 15, No. 1

Klasen, S (2002), "Low Schooling for Girls, Slower Growth for All?, Cross-Country Evidence on the Effect on Gender Inequality in Education on Economic Development", World Bank Economic Review, v. 16, iss. 3, pp. 345-73.

Klasen, S. (2004). In search of the Holy Grail: How to Achieve Pro- Poor Growth? Annual World Bank Conference on Development Economics, The World Bank.

Kosack, S., and Tobin, J. (2006) Funding self-sustaining development: the role of aid, FDI and government in economic success. International Organization, 60, 205—243.

Kolstad, I. and L. Tondel (2002) How do effective social development policies and institutions impcat on the investment climate indeveloping countries?, Social Development Department of the World Bank.

Korinek, Jane (2005), "Trade and Gender: Issues and Interactions", OECD Trade Directorate, OECD Trade Policy Working Papers: 24.

Kraay, A. (2007) Comment, in: Globalization and Poverty. In A. Harrison (Ed.), Globalization and Poverty (pp.134-142). Chicago: The University of Chicago Press.

Krugman, P. R.and M. Obstfeld (1995). Economie Internationale, De Boeck.

Kumar N. and Pradhan J.P. (2002) ''foreign direct investment, externality and economic growth in developing countries: Some empirical explorations and implications for WTO negotiations on investment'' Research and information system, New Delhi India.

Lahimer, N., (2009). La contribution des investissements directs étrangers à la réduction de la pauvreté en Afrique subsaharienne, Université Paris Dauphine

Lam, R. and Wantchekon, L. (2002) Political Dutch Disease, Northwestern University.

Li, Q. and Resnick, A. (2003) "Reversal of Fortunes: Democratic Institutions and Foreign Direct Investment Inflows to Developing Countries", International Organization, vol. 57 n°1, p. 175-211.

Li, X., and Liu, X. (2005) Foreign Direct Investment and Economic Growth: An Increasingly Endogenous Relationship. World Development, 33 (3): 393.407.

Lopez, J. H. (2004) «Pro-poor growth: a review of what we know (and of what we don't).» The World Bank (PRMPR).

Lucas, R. E. (1988) "On the Mechanics of Economic Development," Journal of Monetary Economics, 22, 3–42.

Lucas, R. E. (1990) «Why Doesn't Capital Flow from Rich to Poor Countries» The American Economic Review 80(2): 92-96.

Lui, F.T. (1985) "An Equilibrium Queuing Model of Bribery", *Journal of Political Economy*, vol. 93, n°4, p.760-781.

MacPhail, Fiona and Dong, Xiao-yuan (2007), "Women's Market Work and Household Status in Rural China: Evidence from Jiangsu and Shandong in the Late 1990s", Feminist Economics, v. 13, iss. 3/4, pp. 93-124.

Mallampally, P. and Sauvant, K. P. (1999) 'L'investissement direct étranger dans les pays en développement', Finances & Développement, Vol.36, Numéro 1, pp.10-13.

Markusen, J. R. and Venables A. J. (1999) «Foreign Direct Investment as a catalyst for industrial development « European Economic Review 43: 335-356.

Markusen, J. R. (1995) «The Boundaries of Multinational Entreprises & the Theory of International Trade.» Journal of Economic Perspectives 9(2): 169- 189.

Marwah, K., and Tavakoli, A., (2004) "The Effects of Foreign Capital and Imports on Economic Growth," *Journal of Asian Economics* 15, 399-413.

Matthews, R.C.O. (1986) The economics of institutions and the sources of economic growth, Economic Journal 96 (December), 903-918.

Mayne, M. (1997) Elaboration, microstructure et comportement au fluage de manocomposites Si3N4/SiC, Thèse de doctorats, Université de Limoges.

Mauro, P. (1998) "Corruption and the Composition of Government Expenditure", *Journal of Public Economics*, vol. 69 n°2, p.263-79.

McKern, B. (1993) Transnational Corporations & the Exploitation of Natural Resources, Routledge.

Méon, P.-G. and Sekkat, K. (2005) "Does corruption grease or sand the wheels of growth?", *Public Choice*, vol. 122 n°1-2, p. 69-97.

Méon, P.-G. and Weill, L. (2006) "Is corruption an efficient grease? A cross-country aggregate analysis», presented at the *Public Choice Society Meeting*, New Orleans.

Méon, P.-G. and Sekkat, K. (2007) "Institutional quality and trade: Which institutions? Which trade?", forthcoming in *Economic Inquiry*.

Meon,P.-G. and Sekkat, K. (2007) "Revisiting the Relationship Between Governance and Foreign Direct Investment",DULBEA Working Paper N°07-13.RS

Michalet, C.A. (1999) *« La séduction des nations ou comment attirer les* investissements » Edition Economica.

Mody, A. and Srinivasan K. (1998) "Japanese and U.S. firms as foreign investors: do they march to the same tune?", Canadian Journal of Economics, vol. 31 n°4, p.778-799.

Morisset, J. (2000) "Foreign direct investment in Africa: policies also matter", Transnational Corporations, vol.9 n°2, p.107-125.

Moosa, I. (2002) Foreign Direct Investment: Theory, Evidence and Practice, Palgrave Macmillan.

Moser, G. and T. Ichida (2001) «Economic Growth and Poverty Reduction in Sub-Saharan Africa.» IMF Working Paper(N° 01/112).

Nair-Reichert, U. and Weinhold, D. (2001). «Causality Tests for Cross-Country Panels: a New Look at FDI and Economic Growth in Developing Countries.» Oxford Bulletin of Economics and Statistics 63(2): 153-171.

Narayan, D. and Pritchett L. (1997) Cents and Sociability: household income and social capital in rural Tanzania, Policy Research Working Paper 1–41 (Washington, World Bank).

Narayan, D., Patel R., Schafft,K., Rademacher A. and Koch-Schulte S. (2000) Voices of the Poor. Can Anyone Hear Us? Voices from 46 Countries Washington, DC: The World Bank.

Naude, W. A., and Krugell, W. F. (2003). Managing and developing human resources for attracting foreign direct investment in Africa. Management Dynamics, 12(3), 2—11.

Ndinga, M. M. A. (2002) 'La Gouvernance économique: quelles incidences sur le développement au Congo-Brazzaville?', Conseil pour le Développement de la recherche en sciences sociales en Afrique, Afrique et Développement, Vol. XXVII, Nos.1&2, pp.1-24

Neumayer, E (2003). The Role of Good Governance in the Allocation of Aid, London School of Economics and Political Science (LSE)

Nguyen, T. P. H. (2003). Contribution of Foreign Direct Investment to Poverty Reduction: The Case of Vietnam in the 1990s. In C. Hausen et al. (Eds.), Determinants of Economic Growth and Business Cycles: Theory, Empirical Evidence and Policy Implications. Berlin: Verlag fuer Wissenschaft und Forschung.

Nissanke, M. and E. Thorbecke (2006). «Channels and Policy debate in the globalization inequality- poverty nexus.» World Development 34(8): 1338-1360.

North, D. C. (1990). *Institutions, Institutional Change & Economic Performance*. New York, Cambridge University Press.

OECD (2001), Du bien-être des nations : le rôle du capital humain et social, Paris : OCDE

Ögütçü, M. (2002) *Good Governance and best practices for investment policy and promotion*, (6-7 June 200) Available at: http:// www.oecd.org/dataoecd/36/37/2750363.pdf (Last visited on 4 April 2004).

Paugman, S. (2005) *Les formes élémentaires de la Pauvreté*. Paris, PUF.

Pissarides, C. A. (1997) «Learning by Trading and Returns to Human Capital in Developing Countries.» International Bank for Reconstruction and Development/The World Bank 11(1): 17-32.

Pritchett, L. (1996) «Where has all the growth gone?» World Bank Policy Research Working Paper(N° 1581).

Qian, Nancy (2008), “Missing Women and the Price of Tea in China: The Effect of SexSpecific Earnings on Sex Imbalance”, Quarterly Journal of Economics, v. 126, iss. 3, pp. 1251-1285.

Rama, M. (2001) «Empirical Investment Equations for Developing Countries.» World Bank Publications.

Ravaillon, M. (2004) «Pro-Poor Growth: A primer.» World Bank Policy Research Working Paper: N° 3242.

Ravaillon, M. and Chen, S. (2002) «Measuring pro-poor growth» Economic Letters 78(1): 93-99.

Richards, David and Gelleny, Ronald (2007), “Women's status and economic globalization”, International Studies Quarterly, v. 51, iss. 4, pp. 855-876.

Robertson, C. J. and Watson, A. (2004) «Corruption & Change: The Impact of Foreign Direct Investment.» Strategic Management Journal 25: 385-396.

Rodrik, D. (1999) «Where did all the growth go? External Shocs, Social Conflict, and Growth Collapses.» Journal of Economic Growth 4(4): 385-412.

Rodrik, D., Subramanian, A. and Trebbi, F. (2004) ‘Institutions rule: The primacy of institutions over geography and integration in economic development’ Journal of Economic Growth, 9(2), p.131- 165.

Rose, P. (1995), “Female Education and Adjustment Programs: A Cross-Country Statistical Analysis”, World Development, v. 23, iss. 11, pp. 1931-49.

Sachs, J. D., McArthur, J. W., Schmidt-Traub, G., Kruk, M., Bahadur, C., Faye, M., et al. (2004) Ending Africa’s poverty trap. Brookings Papers on Economic Activity, 1, 117-240.

Saravanamuttoo, N. (1999) “Foreign Direct Investment and Poverty Reduction in Developing Countries”, Turn Course Solutions, Canadian International Development Agency.

Schiller, B. R. (2008) The Economic of Poverty and Discrimination, Pearson.

Seguino, S. (2007) «Is more mobility good? Firm mobility and the low wage-low productivity

Sekkat, K. and Varoudakis, A. (1998) «Exchange-Rate Management and Manufactured Exports in Sub-Saharan Africa» OECD Development Centre Working Papers: N°134.

Sekkat, K. (2004) FDI inflows to the MENA Region: an empirical assessment of the their determinant and impact on development, Brussels: ULB/FEMISE, FEMISE Research Program.

Stiglitz, J. E. (2007) *Making Globalization Work, First edition*, Norton, New York

Skreli, E. (2002) Gouvernance and FDI in Albania, Session V of the Conference Foreign Direct Investment in South East Europe: Implementing Best Policy Practices, Vienna: OECD & Government of Austria. http://www.oecd.org/dataoecd/36/30/2758313.pdf

Sen, A. (1979) «Issues in the Measurement of Poverty» Sc&inavian Journal of Economics 81: 285-307.

Sen, A. (1983) «Poor, Relatively Speaking» Oxford Economic Papers 35: 153-69.

Teal, F. (2000) «Employment & Unemployment in Sub-saharan Africa: An Overview.» Centre for the Study of African Economies, University of Oxford.

Teunissen, J. J., & Akkerman, A. (2006) Africa in the world economy. The national, regional and international challenges. The Hague: FONDAD.

Thomas, Duncan (2000), "Intra-Household Resource Allocation: An Inferential Approach", Journal of Human Resources, v. 35, pp. 635-654.

Todaro, M. P., and Smith, S. C. (2003) *Economic Development*, 8th Edition, Pearson Education Limited, Edinburgh Gate, United Kingdom.

Townsend, P. (1979) «Introduction: Concpets of Poverty & Deprivation» Poverty in United Kingdom: A survey of Household Resources and Standards of Living: 31-60.

Tsai, P.-L. (1995) «Foreign Direct Investment and Income Inequality: Further evidence.» World Development 23(3): 469-483.

Vernon, R. (1971) Sovereignty at Bay. New York, Basic Books.

Vinod, H. D. (2003) "Open Economy and Financial Burden of Corruption: Theory and Application to Asia", *Journal of Asian Economics*, vol. 13 n°6, p. 873–90.

UNCTAD, (1998) World Investment Report 1998: Trends and Determinants, New York & Geneva: United Nations.

UNCTAD (1999) World Investment Report: Foreign Direct Investment and the Challenge of Development, New York, Geneva.

UNCTAD (2006) World Investment Report 2006: FDI from Developing and Transition Economies Implication for Development. New York: United Nations.

UNDP (1997) La bonne gouvernance et le développement durable, New York : PNUD. http://magnet.undp.org/Docs/!UN98-21.PDF/Govfre.htm

Vu, T. B., Gangnes, B., and Noy, I. (2006) "Is Foreign Direct Investment Good for Growth? Answers Using Sectoral Data from China and Vietnam." Unpublished.

Wade, R. (2004) Is Globalization Reducing Poverty and Inequality? World Development, 32(4), 567-589.

Wang, M. (2002) Manufacturing FDI and Economic Growth: Evidence from Asian Economies. Mimeo: University of Oregon Mimeo.

Wei, S.-J. (2000) 'How taxing is corruption on international investors?', Review of Economics and Statistics, Vol. 82, No.1, pp.1-11.

Weinberg, Bruce (2000) "Computer Use and the Demand for Female Workers", Industrial and Labor Relations Review, v. 53, iss. 2, pp. 290-307.

Welch, Finis (2000) "Growth in Women's Relative Wages and in Inequality Among Men: One Phenomenon or Two?", American Economic Review, v. 90, iss. 2, pp. 444-449.

Wilhelms, S. K.S. and Dean, M. S. W. (1998) Foreign Direct Investment and its determinants in emerging economies, Washington D.C.: USAID & Bureau for Africa/Office of Sustainable Development, Discussion Paper No.9.

World Bank (2000) «World Development Report 2000/2001: Attacking Poverty» Washington, D.C:

World Bank, (2003) «World Development Report 2003, Washington, D.C.

Xu,,D. and Shenkar, O. (2002). «Institutional distance and the multinational entreprise.» The Academy of Management Review 27(4): 608-618.

Yeaple, S. R. (2003) «The complex integration strategies of multinationals and cross dependencies in the structure of foreign direct investment.» Journal of International Economics 60(2): 293-314.

Zhang, K. H. (2001) "How does foreign direct investment affect economic growth in China?" Economics of Transition, 9(3):679-693.